THE PLAY OF THE WEATHER

AND

OTHER TUDOR COMEDIES

THE PLAY
OF THE WEATHER

by JOHN HEYWOOD

AND OTHER TUDOR COMEDIES

Adapted into Modern English
by
MAURICE HUSSEY
and
SURENDRA AGARWALA

THEATRE ARTS BOOKS

NEW YORK

Published by
Theatre Arts Books
333 Sixth Avenue
New York, New York 10014

Printed in Great Britain
Cox & Wyman Ltd
London, Reading and Fakenham

CONTENTS

PREFACE

The comedies in this volume include the best known of the 'Interludes' of the early sixteenth century. Since there are no easily accessible editions of four out of five of these plays, we have decided to prepare a collection suitable for reading or acting today. The plays would, for example, prove an excellent conclusion to an amateur bill of medieval mystery plays.

The originals appeared in a spelling that is unacceptable today. The Pothecary's lie (see p. 71), as it stood without punctuation in the first edition, is a single example:

> Now marke for here begynneth the reuell
> This tampion flew x longe myle leuell
> To a faire castell of lyme and stone
> For strength I knowe nat such a one
> Which stode vpon an hyll full hye
> At fote wherof a ryuer ranne bye.

In our modernization we have been obliged to reduce long speeches to a manageable compass, to suppress a number of indecencies, and to shorten very repetitive exchanges of dialogue. Outbursts of song and dance that cannot be adequately re-created and are quite unnecessary to the unfolding of the play have likewise been jettisoned.

Virtually everything here was originally written in rhymed couplets, varying irregularly from seven to ten syllables in a line. It is hoped, however, that the language retains at times a slightly archaic flavour and stateliness. This is valuable since it suggests a period, without causing a hindrance in the process.

Finally, we should like to thank Dr T. W. Craik of the English Department of Aberdeen University, the chief authority on this subject, for his advice at the outset.

Cambridge, April 1967

S.K.A.
M.P.H.

INTRODUCTION

OLD ENGLISH COMEDIES

It is well known that the oldest popular plays presented in England were religious: the Mystery Plays which depicted stories from the Bible. To our best knowledge these plays were regularly performed in many English cities and existed in very many different versions. It is also understood that the version acted in a city like Chester or York, for instance, altered as years went by. The earliest of our English mystery cycles of plays, that acted in Chester, is a particularly serious account of biblical events. Even here, however, there is a little comedy interwoven with the drama. It is in the later mystery plays associated with the Yorkshire town of Wakefield that we find a good deal of incidental comedy.

We might take an example from the Wakefield plays. The first great comic character in them is Mrs Noah, about whom the Bible is almost totally silent. The unknown writer saw her as a perfect hindrance to her carpenter-husband, an example of the nagging wife that is known as the Shrew. Here, for example, is her refusal to go on board the new ark. We sense that she is rather overstating her case and that she is sure to have to give way:

MRS NOAH: No one ever barred me up, no, not in all my life
In such a little cage.
There's hardly room to turn.[1]

But when the water begins to rise around her she admits the wisdom of having an ark to turn to:

So now in your fine ship right quickly come I,
For fear that I drown here.

[1] Quotations are taken from Dennis Hamley's verson in *Three Towneley Plays* (Kingswood Plays Series).

Once Mrs Noah is reunited with her husband, she does not fall into his arms, as we might expect. Instead they start fighting – known then as *flyting*:

NOAH: I'll make you shut up, you cause of all our troubles.
I'll break body and bone, until your blood bubbles.

They carry on in this way until the rains are too heavy and the biblical story can wait no longer for their personal squabbles. This section of the play provides an example of what is known as *comic relief*. Some modern critics seem to think that it is for this kind of comedy that the Mystery Plays were written, but this is surely not the case. It is excellent to have a Mrs Noah, but she is of no importance to the story. She is there to provide a moment's breathing space intended to send us back to the story proper with fresh relish – so that the basic idea can stand out the more seriously after the decrease in tension. The main purpose of the Flood play is to show the way in which God chose Noah and his ark as a way of saving mankind.

The plays in this volume are of a particular type. About 1500 there grew up short self-contained plays for boy actors known then and now as Interludes. Some were humorous but others were moral and even scientific in theme and all of them were designed for young performers, the Boy in *The Play of the Weather* being the youngest of all. The gentry who were hosts to the performers probably joined in the acting. In fact, there were over fifteen companies of actors supported by the nobility.

Towards the end of the sixteenth century, however, these Interludes were being forgotten. A late example is *Jack Juggler*, anonymous but thought to be the work of Nicholas Udall, headmaster of Eton. When there were groups of professionals equipped with London theatres, as in the last quarter of the century, there was less need for itinerant acting. The master of comedy at that period was, of course, William Shakespeare and it seems that he may well have known incidents from the Interludes. *Jack Juggler* might have been part of the inspiration for his comic Autolycus in *The Winter's Tale* and behind the twin situation in *The Comedy of Errors*. In *A Midsummer Night's Dream* the inclusion of a group of rustic actors is the professional actor's satire upon the amateur drama and a complete Interlude in itself.

Finally, we should not forget the old folk plays about St George or Robin Hood which were acted by local amateurs everywhere. Henry VIII is known to have enjoyed performing in the role of Robin, though in middle age only the role of Friar Tuck would have been at all suitable for him. Last of all, there were short playlets with songs and dancing now known as Elizabethan Jigs which were given at the end of a professional company's programme to send the audience away in a good frame of mind. Their subjects range from wooing to beating, with quarrels and misunderstandings all the while. The difference between a Jig and an Interlude is that the latter offers a complete after-dinner entertainment. It is an independent dramatic form which naturally stands on its own.

JOHN HEYWOOD

Chronological Table

1497 April	Heywood born in London.
1509 to 1513–14	Choirboy in Chapel Royal.
1514	Attended Oxford, probably not for more than one term.
1515 to 1519	No records, but probably at court, serving as a musician.
1519 to 1521	Mentioned in records as having received quarterly wages of 100s. for services as a court singer.
1521 to 1528	Period of dramatic writing? Receives some land from the king and is paid regularly as a musician.

1527	*The Play of the Weather* written?
1529	*Four PP's, John John, The Pardoner and the Friar* written?
1529	Latest date of marriage to Eliza Rastell.
1533	William Rastell, brother of Heywood's wife, prints *The Pardoner and the Friar, The Play of the Weather*.
1534 February	William Rastell prints *John John*.
1545?	*Four PP's* printed.
1578 June?	Heywood dies in exile at Louvain, France.

The details of Heywood's life after the publication of his plays are not of immediate concern to us here. One or two of the more important events of his life after 1533 are dealt with in the account of John Heywood that follows.

When or where John Heywood was born is not known precisely. The events and the course of his life have to be pieced together from a variety of sources. This fact is surprising in a man who was so distinguished in his lifetime. His life crossed the paths of four monarchs: Henry VIII, Edward VI, and the Queens Mary and Elizabeth. His talents as a musician and playwright brought him into contact with Renaissance scholars from some of the noblest households in the country. He himself married into an illustrious family: his wife's uncle was Sir Thomas More, Chancellor of England. Like Sir Thomas More, Heywood had to fight most of his life to remain a Catholic. At the end of his life he was in exile for his religious convictions and he died abroad. (The history of Sir Thomas More's persecution and struggle has been dramatized in the play *A Man For All Seasons* by Robert Bolt.) Heywood's grandson was John Donne, who made a better reputation for himself as a poet than Heywood had made as a dramatist.

It is thought that Heywood was born in London in 1497 and he is believed to have been a choirboy in the Chapel Royal for some five years, between 1509 and 1514. He probably went to Oxford after that, but for little more than a term. He does not seem to have liked Oxford, and he returned to London to serve as a musician at the court of Henry VIII. During this time he doubled as a court singer. Internal details from his plays suggest that they were written between 1521 and 1528, while he was receiving regular pay as a player of the virginal, a type of harpsichord.

Heywood's early life closely follows the development of theatrical companies out of choirs like the Chapel Royal. Heywood is known to have performed an Interlude with 'his children' before Princess Mary in 1538. This does not mean that Heywood's sons and daughters acted, but that a company of boys performed the Interlude. This company might have been formed out of the Chapel Royal choir or out of the choir of St Paul's Cathedral. The Chapel Royal choir, for example, had from 24 to 38 men and from 8 to 12 children. This choir, like the 'Paul's boys' has a history which began with performances of religious music, and then provided musical entertainments having little to do with religion. Finally, it became a mere band of acting boys. It is very likely that Heywood was what we would now call the 'producer' and 'actor-manager' for one of these two bands of acting children. In *The Play of the Weather* the appearance of Little Dick is little more than capitalizing on the youngest member of the company. Alternatively, Heywood could have called on the services of an independent organization of boy actors such as was run by Udall, the probable author of *Jack Juggler*.

But Heywood's life was not entirely taken up with playing music and writing and performing his own interludes. In the spring of 1543 he was implicated in a Catholic plot to overthrow the Protestant Archbishop Cranmer. He was imprisoned, and in 1544 was charged with treason, his property was confiscated, and he awaited sentence. However, he was more or less miraculously pardoned, his lands were restored to him and he appears to have regained royal favour. There was a brief period of respite for English Catholics under Queen Mary, for whom Heywood always had a high regard. But four years after the Protestant Elizabeth came to the throne, Heywood went into exile – in 1562. We hear of him fourteen years later in 1576, when he is admitted into a Jesuit college at Antwerp. In 1578 there were religious disorders in that town and the Jesuits, including Heywood, were made prisoners by a Protestant mob. Heywood fled to Louvain in France, where he died in June of the same year.

Heywood's dramatic work is an isolated and significant watershed between medieval drama and the later Elizabethan drama. Four of the six plays generally attributed to Heywood appear here. In short, they move away from medieval drama in three main elements:

(i) Farce, which was incidental to the miracle plays and the moralities and was used largely to make otherwise dull material palatable, is now of first importance to the interlude;

(ii) Characters portrayed are individuals, recognizable as being unique and specific, whereas they had been Biblical or simply representative and undistinguished as individuals in former drama;

(iii) The familiar medieval debate held in intellectual circles has become a poetic and dramatic art form.

In *The Play of the Weather* the element of farce is very strong. Merry-Report especially contributes to the irreverence shown towards Jupiter. Though Heywood avoids using the kind of direct preaching that we have in *The Pardoner and the Friar*, the play makes a noteworthy attempt to deal with some justifiable grievances. But in the end it asserts Jupiter's (Henry VIII's?) authority and ability to unite his angry subjects. The dramatic quality of *The Pardoner and the Friar* is made up of ordinary dialogue and horse-play and it is thought to be an early work. The reference to Pope Leo suggests that the play was written earlier than 1521. It was Pope Leo X who had authorized the sale of indulgences. The sermons that the Pardoner and the Friar give are obviously mock-sermons, but those who are not interested in even these are to be entertained by the riot at the end. The *Four P's* is less dramatic than either *The Play of the Weather* or *John John*, but it is one of the most humorous. The characters here are quite firmly delineated and come as forceful individuals. Since this play needs virtually no stage properties, we can assume that it was most likely performed at a court dinner when entertainment was required. *John John* is the furthest removed from previous drama and is an animated domestic farce. Though *John John* may not be as appealing as *The Play of the Weather*, it is a sophisticated product for the 1520's. With this play we notice a distinct movement towards realism; human beings are no longer looked at as a group, but as individuals with human failings and characteristics. John Heywood must be seen as more than just a writer of some dramatic trifles which are often farcical, seemingly spontaneous and just a little mad. In the self-addressed poem that follows it will be seen that Heywood's estimation was much like our own:

> Art thou Heywood with the mad, merry wit?
> Yes, forsooth, master, that same is even hit.
> Art thou Heywood that applieth mirth more than thrift?
> Yea sir, I take merry mirth a golden gift.
> Art thou Heywood that hath made many mad plays?
> Yea, many plays, few good works in all my days.
> Art thou Heywood that hath made men merry long?
> Yea, and will if I be made merry among.
> Art thou Heywood that would be made merry now?
> Yea sir: help me to it now, I beseech you.

THE PLAY OF THE WEATHER

CHARACTERS

JUPITER, *a god*

MERRY-REPORT, *a vice*

THE GENTLEMAN

THE MERCHANT

THE RANGER

THE WATER-MILLER

THE WIND-MILLER

THE GENTLEWOMAN

THE LAUNDRESS

A SMALL BOY

Attendants

SCENE: an open space with a throne in the centre of a raised dais at the back of the stage – Entrances left and right and front of stage, through auditorium.

THE PLAY OF THE WEATHER

The Play of the Weather is possibly the most enchanting of all Tudor Interludes. A major element of the Interludes in this book is the verbal fun; bitter argument between characters is also important. In *The Play of the Weather* the argument has become petitioning, and the petitioning is for something quite English – the weather. The weather, and the control of it was a subject that was debated in the court of Henry VIII. This fact, along with a number of details about the weather and its effects on the crops during the 1520's, helps us to date the play as having been written around 1527. A historical approach to all these plays is useful: here it is most rewarding.

It is important to remember that John Heywood was a member of Henry VIII's court during this time, between 1523 and 1528. The king had to listen to petitions himself and it would not be surprising to learn that spectators of Heywood's play identified Jupiter with Henry. The play does not in fact need such an explanation, for it is complete, comic and self-explanatory. But there is reasonable ground for thinking that Jupiter is, in some respects, Henry VIII. In the language of the Tudors, the king was a giver of 'all manner weathers'. The king, compared to his subjects, was as the rain to earth: he was the source of goodness and plenty, the nourisher of flowers, trees and corn.

It is an ingenious idea to have a number of people petitioning Jupiter for particular kinds of weather which would favour them or their trades. As such the play is a superb comedy. At the same time it is something of a comment on early Tudor England, whose economic (and religious) troubles were grounded in greed and pride.

Without exception, Heywood's representative group of people all show pride in one way or another. It is no wonder that Jupiter brings a serious note into the play when he points out the need for co-operation between tradesmen. The petitioners are over-whelmingly concerned with their own interests:

(i) The Gentleman petitions for his recreation (mainly hunting);
(ii) the Merchant, perhaps rightly, assumes that his importance to the country will gain him admittance to the god;
(iii) the greedy and ill-mannered Ranger pushes forward, trying to get past Merry-Report, thinking he can get immediate satisfaction in this way;
(iv) the Water-Miller is just as thoughtless and disrespectful;
(v) the Wind-Miller is not only discontented, but also full of self-pity;
(vi) when faced with the audience, the Gentlewoman pretends to be timid– but she soon reveals that she is conceited;
(vii) the Laundress is jealous of beauty in others and, again perhaps rightly, despises the nobility for their time-wasting;
(viii) the Boy thinks that he can *buy* whatever weather he wants.

Another point that is worth bearing in mind is that the characters actually *say* that they are representing people like themselves. The Merchant speaks for all merchants; the Ranger and the Millers for all the members of *their* respective trades. The Gentlewoman speaks for all those who want to keep their beautiful complexions, and the Laundress for all those who work away hard without respite. The Boy has been sent along by a street gang as its best spokesman.

Heywood has chosen an interesting variety of trades to portray. The Merchant, as well as the first audience of the Interlude, acknowledges the importance of trading with foreign countries in the 1520's. The merchant class supplied England with all manner of goods which the country could not otherwise obtain. The Ranger was a gamekeeper or forester who was usually appointed by the king to look after the royal forests and grounds, along with their wild animals. A ranger would be paid an ordinary salary for his work. But it was well known that rangers normally supplemented their incomes by collecting fallen dead wood which they took to neighbouring towns to sell as firewood. The trouble was that when there was no dead wood for them to collect, rangers would quite happily cut down the healthy trees that they were supposed to look after and sell them as firewood. This happened so much that in 1540 an investigation was made into the activities of the forest-keepers, and as a result of the findings, many rangers were dismissed. As for the Millers, their greed had been proverbial since Chaucer's day and the quarrel about whether a watermill was better than a windmill would come as no surprise. The Gentlewoman and the Laundress are obviously opposed in interests: the Laundress has a legitimate complaint against the Gentlewoman's wasteful way of spending her time.

Little Dick, the Boy, is a special case. Child-actors, playing children, were always popular on the Tudor stage. Boys did, of course, play various parts and would always play women on the stage. An acting company would usually include a few boys. Little Dick is particularly attractively presented and he really does talk like a boy who has just come off the street. The part should be played by the youngest and smallest of boys: in the original edition of the Interlude, after his name in the list of characters comes the famous phrase '*the least that can play*'.

There is only the buffoon Merry-Report, the link-man, left. He is the only person to come forward in answer to Jupiter's request for a crier and he knows the formula 'Oyez, oyez' with which to practise. In other sixteenth-century plays in which Jupiter appears his companion is always Mercury, the messenger of the gods, with wings on his ankles. Merry-Report has something of this nature, though he owes his name to his light-hearted manner of speech. He shows no concern at all in the outcome of the weather-petitions and has no other axe to grind. He tries, however, to disrupt the order of things and has something of the old character of the theatrical Vice who started his dramatic life as a devil and ended as a comic personality.

He shares a sense of his self-importance with everybody else in the play – even Jupiter. He is surprised that nobody bows down to him and laughs at the amount of trust that the petitioners put in his goodwill:

> I pray you mark the fashion of this honest man: [Merchant]
> He puts more trust in me at one meeting here
> Than he shall find reason why for many a year.

Little Dick actually thinks him 'master god' which may account for a slight tenderness in Merry-Report's attitude towards him. In the end, however, he cannot see the sense in following up the petitions of such 'fools and boys', none of whom has done more than promise him a reward. Yet it also falls to him alone to see clearly what has happened when the petitions have all been granted. In a line that must be spoken with great emphasis he sums the whole play up:

> Now we shall have the weather just as ever it was.

The Play of the Weather in performance is extremely effective. All that is needed is the royal throne on a dais and a few properties for Jupiter. A good start to the play can be given by simply having a modern weather chart (such as is familiar to every television viewer) on display as a backcloth. Jupiter could be given a desk with charts and compasses. Among the kit there can be the new moon referred to on p. 27. and although it is an anachronism, a large globe can be displayed. There is no need to divide Jupiter from the rest by a curtain, as long as the actors never allow themselves to take any notice of him unless they have been ceremoniously admitted to his presence by Merry-Report.

The dressing of all eight petitioners may be either simple or ingenious. The Ranger should have an axe, the Gentleman a horn and at least one of the Millers ought to be a genuine Dusty. With a lively, busy and springy Merry-Report who controls the pace of the performance and a dignified speaker for Jupiter, a performance of this Interlude should always prove highly entertaining.

JUPITER *pronounces from his throne:*
     Far too long would it take to recite
     The ancient estate wherein I have reigned,
     The honour, the praise given me as of right,
     What glory I have had, fully unfeigned,
     From each creature whom duty has constrained.
     For above all gods, since father Saturn's fall,
     I, Jupiter, am ever principal.

     Before my presence, in my high parliament,
     Both gods and goddesses of all degrees
     Have late assembled, by common assent,
     For the redress of certain enormities,
     Bred among them through extremities,
     Inflicted by each on the other and on all,
     And now to name them these in especial:

     Our father, cold Saturn; warm Phoebus;
     Windy Aeolus, and rainy Phoebe by name,
     Whose contrary natures so far oppose
     And whose malice each other does defame.
     All four have abused, quite out of frame,
     The due round of heavenly constellations
     To the great damage of all earthly nations.

     They have, in conclusion, wholly surrendered
     Into my hands, as much concerning
     All kinds of weather which they engendered,
     With all their powers for time everlasting
     To bring here such order as suited my pleasing.
     This thing, on my part no action required
     But to show to each party what right desired.

So now to finish the rest of my intent
For which I earthwards now have descended
Is only to satisfy and content
All manner of people who have been offended
By any foul weather that ought to be amended.
Upon their complaints, declaring their grief,
I shall fashion a remedy for their relief.

And to give knowledge of my hither resort
I require this proclaimed should be
To all the people by one from this court
Whom I shall choose from those that I see.

JUPITER *advances from his throne towards the audience;* MERRY-
REPORT *comes forward from the back of the auditorium and mounts
the stage.*

Therefore each man advance, and let me see
Which of you is most apt to be our crier.

MERRY-R: Now, I beseech you my lord, look on me first.
I trust your lordship shall not find me the worst.

JUPITER: Why! what are you that approach so near?

MERRY-R (*easing forward*): In truth, so please your lordship, it is I.

JUPITER: What kind of man are you, tell quickly.

MERRY-R: By god, a poor gentleman who lives near by.

JUPITER: But what are you called where you resort?

MERRY-R: In truth, my lord, Master Merry-Report.

JUPITER: You are no fit man for my business,
I need a man who shows far more wiseness.

MERRY-R: Why, cannot your lordship like my manner,
My apparel, nor my name neither?

JUPITER: To none of these am I devoted.

MERRY-R (*aside*): A proper likelihood of being promoted!
Well then, as wise as you seem to be,
Yet can you see no wiseness in me.
But since you dispraise me as too stupid an elf,
I pray you give me leave to praise myself.

For as I be saved if I shall not lie,
I saw no man sue for the office but I!

If you take me not now, and I go,
You must soon, whether you will or no.
And since your care is but for the weathers,
What matters if my apparel be fur or feathers?
As for my name: reporting always truly,
What harm to report a sad matter merely?
He addresses the audience.
What man can compare, or show a like comfort,
As is ever shown by me, Merry-Report?
And as to the work you at this time intend,
To all your weathers I am indifferent.
*He begins to bound about the stage and gestures more wildly to
illustrate his remarks.*
I care not be it dull or bright,
Sunlight, moonlight, starlight, twilight, torchlight.
Cold, heat, mist, dry, hail, rain, frost, thunder;
Cloudy, misty, windy, fair, foul overhead or under.
Temperate, intemperate: whatever it be,
I promise your lordship all is one to me.
He looks pleased with himself and bows to Jupiter in expectation.
JUPITER: Well, son, considering your indifferency,
And hearing the rest of your declaration,
I make you my servant. Now immediately
I wish you to depart and make proclamation,
Publicizing my pleasure to every nation;
Which thing once done, with all diligence
Make your return again to my presence.

Here shall I greet suitors of each degree;
And such as seem to you in most desert to be
I will have them brought before my majesty.
As for the rest that are not so worthy

Make your report to me equally.
Then I may hear every suit in full.
Off with you at speed, with no more lull.

MERRY-R: Now, good my lord god, Our Lady be with you!

MERRY-REPORT *departs to proclaim Jupiter's offer – stage left.*

JUPITER: Since I have this far declared my intents
I will withdraw awhile my godly presence.

JUPITER *draws a curtain (actual or imaginary) around himself and the throne area.* MERRY-REPORT *returns.*

MERRY-R (*addressing audience*): Now sirs, take heed, for here comes god's servant!

Pauses and looks expectantly for their reactions.

By your faith, have you neither cap nor knee?
Will not one of you bow down to me?
Do you count for nothing my authority?
No 'Welcome home' nor 'Where have you been?'
Nor 'It is a long time since you were last seen.'
For, on my faith, I think in my conscience
I've been as far from here as heaven is from hence.
To London and to Lombardy,
To Baldock and to Barbary,
To Canterbury and Coventry and Colchester,
To Guildford and Gotham and Gloucester.
The devil himself, without more leisure,
Could not have gone half so far, I am sure!
But now I have informed them, let them choose,
For indeed, I care not who win or who lose.

A horn is sounded offstage by the GENTLEMAN *who then enters with his attendants, stage left.*

MERRY-R: Now, by my faith, that was a good sound.

GENTLEMAN (*to the audience*): Good-morrow to my friends everyone.

MERRY-R: Say that to me and leave the rest alone!
Sir, you are welcome with all your men.

MERRY-REPORT *bows formally to the* GENTLEMAN *who is looking for signs of Jupiter's presence.*

GENTLEMAN: Now, in good truth, I must ask you then
    Since I meet you here by this chance
    I beg to have with you more acquaintance.
    I would ask your advice upon a great matter:
    I come here to sue to the great god Jupiter
    For help in matters concerning my chief recreation,
    According to his recent proclamation.

MERRY-R: Indeed, sir. Stand here and hold fast awhile.
    This shall all be done in the quickest style.

He approaches Jupiter's throne.

    My lord, a suitor stands here, just behind.
    He has come to speak out his mind.

JUPITER: Whatever he desires, let him appear.

MERRY-REPORT *returns and collects the Gentleman. He leads him towards the throne and retreats but remains listening attentively at the side.*

MERRY-R: Now good Sir Gentleman, I pray you come near,
    Come now this way to the great Jupiter.

GENTLEMAN: Most mighty prince and god of every nation;
    Will your highness grant full hearing
    To one who, according to your proclamation,
    Appears before you humbly and bows pleading?

He bows to Jupiter.

    Not for myself alone I speak, but widely
    For all sprung of noble and ancient stock.
    They above all do most thankfully
    Take pains for the welfare of the simpler flock.
    This, great god, is our whole desire:
    For the ease of our mind and frame
    We take to the hunting-field with fire
    And plead for good weather for our game.
    Dry and not misty, the wind calm and still,
    That after our hounds running so merrily

We may follow over dale and hill.

JUPITER: Right well do I perceive your whole request,
Which shall not fail to rest in memory.
There I wish that you set your mind at rest
Till I have heard what other men would tell to me.

JUPITER *dismisses the* GENTLEMAN *who departs, speaking these lines and bowing once more to the god.*

GENTLEMAN: In heaven and earth, honoured be the name
Of Jupiter, who in his godly goodness
Has set this matter in such good frame
That every man shall be satisfied, doubtless.
And first for us nobles and gentlemen
I doubt not that his wisdom will provide
Such weather that in our hunting, now and then,
We may both chase and game on every side.

MERRY-R (*advancing*): Concerning your suit here, depart when
it please you:
For you may be sure, as I can, I shall help you.

GENTLEMAN: Then give me your hand. That promise I take.
And if on my behalf any suit you make
I promise your work will be repaid
More handsomely than now shall be said.

The GENTLEMAN *leaves the scene, (stage right).* MERRY-REPORT *watches his departure. Meanwhile, from the opposite side the* MERCHANT *in a long cloak makes his way on to the set.*

MERRY-R: Master Parson, by the cloak. You are welcome.

MERCHANT: Parson? No sir. I come to be suitor
Please bring me before great Jupiter.

MERRY-R: Yes, that I can and will do it indeed.
Tarry while I make way for you with speed.

Advances to the throne of Jupiter bowing.

Sire, yonder is another man in place
Who makes great suit to speak with your grace.
Your pleasure he awaits. When known,
He seeks to step to your majestic throne.

JUPITER: Bring him to my presence with no delay.

MERRY-REPORT *leads the Merchant to Jupiter. Bowing low before the god he speaks.*

MERCHANT: Most mighty prince, lord of lords all,
  I humbly beseech your majesty
  For merchant men in every port of call
  That it may please you in your charity
  First, to consider the worthiness of our request:
  What wealth we bring the rest with care and strife.
  So then to reward us as you shall think best.
  In the daily danger of our goods and life
  We freight from home things that are in plenty
  And home we bring such goods as here be scant.
  Who should before us merchants accounted be?
  Without us the world would wish and want.
  We seek to establish such weather, your grace:
  No storm or mist, a wind measurable
  So that we may move well from place to place
  Rigging our sails for speed most valuable.
  And we would the wind may change and turn
  East, West, North and South as best may be set
  That we are not in one place too long to sojourn
  For the length of our voyage our costs may forfeit.

JUPITER: Full well have you spoken and I accept it so,
  And so shall I reward you before I go hence.
  But you must have patience till I have heard more
  Since I must impartially give sentence.

The MERCHANT *bows himself away from the throne.* MERRY-REPORT *immediately pounces upon him.*

MERRY-R: Now sir, by your faith, if you should be sworn,
  Heard you ever god speak so since you were born?
  So wisely, so gently his words do come!

MERCHANT: I thank his grace. My suit is safe home.

MERRY-R: Sir, what voyage do you intend next to take?
  For then, by Our Lady, what wealth you will make!

Till then you and I on our rounds must part;
I will do much for you, have no fear in your heart.

MERCHANT: Sir, if you remember me when the time shall come,
Though I repay not all, I shall hand you a sum.

The MERCHANT *leaves, (stage right).*

MERRY-R: Now, fare you well, and God thank you, by St
      Anne.

(*To audience*) I pray you mark the fashion of this honest man:
He puts more trust in me at one meeting here
Than he shall find reason why for many a year.

The RANGER *comes from behind* MERRY-REPORT (*stage left*) *and
comes right down towards the audience.*

RANGER: God be with you! Christ bless this company!

MERRY-R: In faith you are welcome; (*aside*) though very
      scantily.

Sir, for this visit what is your matter?

RANGER: I would now speak with the god Jupiter.

MERRY-R: That cannot be. But you may do this:
Tell me your mind – I am an officer of his.

RANGER: Is that so? I beg you mercy.
Your worship may think me unmannerly.
So please your grace, it is thus as you see:
I come for myself and many others like me.
All rangers and keepers of such places
As forest and parks, purlieus and chases,
Where we protect all manner of game.
Small is our profit and great comes the blame.
And our chief profit from windfallen trees.
Alas, it is our pain that there are few of these.
This is the thing in which we find grief
And the reason I come is to sue for relief:
That the god, taking pity on hearing all this,
Will send us good winds with bluster and hiss.
But if I cannot get god to do us some good,
I will hire the devil to run through the wood:

The roots to turn up and the tops to crash under
And a mischief upon them and lightning and thunder.

MERRY-R: Well said! You care not who win or who lose
So long as you find ways for living and food.

RANGER: I pray, let me pass you—

The RANGER *tries to approach the throne but finds his way barred by Merry-Report.*

MERRY-R: Why no, sir. By my faith you—

RANGER: If not, I will leave you just as I found you.

MERRY-R: Go when you want. No one will hound you.

The RANGER *goes out, (stage left) and the* WATER-MILLER *comes from the opposite corner.*

WATER-MILLER: No water have we to grind up our stint,
The wind is so strong that the rain cannot fall,
It keeps our mill dams as dry as a flint
And we are undone; we grind nothing at all.
The greater is the pity, it seems well to me
That no use to man is his field full of corn
Till it is ground up by such millers as we.
Indeed, to come to ourselves, we are but drudges,
And beggars, no less, apart from our toll
Which is but small though everyone grudges
For the grist of a bushel the cost of a quart-bowl.
Then, but for our repairs we might do well:
Our millstones, our wheel with its cogs and trindle,[1]
Our floodgate, our millpool, our water-wheel,
Our hopper, our axle and our iron spindle.
Therefore my need has driven me here,
To sue in this as I must now openly:
Rain in plenty god Jupiter so dear,
And on to your presence I step most boldly.

MERRY-REPORT *bars the way though the Water-Miller has grown passionate in his declaration.*

MERRY-R: Sir, I do not doubt your audacity,

[1] *Trindle,* lantern-wheel

But I am afraid you lack the capacity.
For, if you were wise, you could well see
How badly you err on the score of courtesy.

WATER-MILLER (*to audience*): All you here note this man well:
(*To Merry-Report*) Remember this, sir: you should never tell
Your equal so knavish a thing. Nor should you slight
Your brother who is like to seek a fight.

MERRY-R: You are neither brother nor friend to me,
For I am god's servant, can you not see?

WATER-MILLER: Ah, indeed by the devil and his dam
I took you for a knave just as I am.
But if you are what you claim to be
I must and will obey your authority.
So, since I may not speak with Jupiter,
I beseech you to be my solicitor.

MERRY-R: As for that, I will be your well-wisher.
I see that you are a water-miller,
And your whole design, as I understand the matter
Is for plenty of rain to increase the water.
This is prevented, you declare resolutely,
Only by the wind, your mortal enemy.

WATER-MILLER: That is so: it blows so hard aloft
We never have rain, or at most not oft.
And so I ask you, put in the god's mind
To banish for ever all strong wind.

As he is at the climax of his speech, the WIND-MILLER *comes upon the scene* (*stage right*).

WIND-MILLER: A wind-miller am I, like many besides me.
No wretch in misery is as wretched as we!
Those of my craft are all wiped out at once
The wind is weak it stirs not our stones.
The rain never stops, too long last the showers:
They pour all day long through twenty-four hours.
End when it will, at night or at noon,

Another storm starts when that one is done.
Such a quantity of rain, you know well enough,
Diminishes the wind even though it is rough.

He beats his breast in an act of self-pity.

A miller! Oh, a plague and mischief!
Who would be a miller? As good be a thief!
Yet, time was when grinding was in plenty,
Who then were such good fellows as we?
As fast as god made corn, we turned it into food,
Who could be less spared from the common good?
But let that point pass – for I fear our pride
Is the cause of the adversity which god does provide.
And so I submit myself in order to see
What comfort may come from humility.
And now, at this place, they said in the cry
The god has come down to grant remedy.

MERRY-R: There is no doubt he is here, on that throne;
But as for your complaint he trusts me alone.
And I see that from what you say in that complaint
Inclemency of rain does make the wind too faint
That you wind-millers are almost washed away.

WIND-MILLER: If Jupiter does not help, it is as you say,
For in my wish I cannot falter.
Oh, that in this world there were no drop of water
Nor ever rain but wind continual.
Then we wind-millers would be lords over all!

MERRY-REPORT *listens to this challenging speech and then points
out the Water-Miller who has been growing incredulous and irritated
to find his own desires so completely overturned.*

MERRY-R: Come on and see how you two can agree:
A brother of yours, a miller, as you be!

WATER-MILLER: According to our crafts we may be brothers,
But while be both live we shall never be lovers.
We are of one craft, but not of one kind:
I live by water and he by the wind.

MERRY-REPORT *slips away behind the throne of the god and leaves the two millers face to face.*

While you, sir, want wind continually
I would like to have rain fall endlessly.
But by experience we may both well see
That seldom together can these two be.
As long as wind howls, it is quite plain,
Ten to one you will get not a drop of rain:
And when the firmament is too oppressed
Down comes the rain and sets the wind to rest.
From this you see we cannot both obtain
For you will have wind while I must have rain.

They stand together advancing towards the audience.

And so, I think that before this audience
We should plead our case or part from hence.
He who is thought weakest when we have finished,
Should leave his suit and agree to be banished.

WIND-MILLER: Agreed (*they shake hands*) since water and wind
   are our suit
Which should be spared we will first dispute.
For examples, to the sea I now resort
Where ships by means of wind sail from port to port,
From land to land distances of many a mile;
The voyage is great and small is the while.
Now, since the wind is conveyer of all,
Who but the wind should have thanks above all?

WATER-MILLER: The wind can do nothing – a simple matter –
Unless the ships float upon the water.
But on water you may, without any wind,
Row your vessel where you have a mind.
Nothing more can please the mariner
Than mild gusts of wind with plenty of water.
For commonly the cause of every shipwreck
Is excess of wind when the water did lack.
In the teeth of storms the peril is such

That no wind were better than far too much.

WIND-MILLER: Well, if my reasoning here does not stand,
I will forsake the sea and jump to land.
And now to my mind a proverb does come:
'One bushel of March dust is worth a king's ransom.'
Whereas the rain never does good but hurt,
The wind only makes dust, while water makes dirt.
And, in every church, where god's service is,
The organs bear the brunt of half the choir,
Is this not a wind-blown sound, or am I a liar?
Fill me a bagpipe with your water full
As sweetly shall it sound as if stuffed with wool!

WATER-MILLER: On my faith, I think the moon is at the full
For frank fancies are then so plentiful.
But sir, I pray you, give me a moment
And I will answer to your whole comment.
Imagine one summer's day without wind to be,
And raging wind on winter days some two or three;
Much more shall dry that one calm day in summer
Than shall those three windy days in winter.
Thank the wind? never. Thank chiefly the sun.
Him shall we thank for all this when all is done.
Now, oft the wind so flattens the corn on the spot
That it never can ripe, can only rot.
But now, sir, I deny your main principle
If drought went on, it were impossible
To have any grain; for, ere it can grow
You must plough your land, harrow and sow,
Which will not be unless you may have rain,
To grow and to ripen all kinds of crop
You must have water or they must all drop.
For cleansing all filth, too, for washing, scouring
Water is essential to help our whole existing.
In brewing, baking and cooking of meat,
Without any water, what could you drink or eat?

We cannot live without water, neither man nor beast,
For water sustains both us and the least.
And so for that wind you here sue for
It's good for your windmill and for no more!

WIND-MILLER: My windmill can grind more corn in an hour
Than your watermill can in three or four.
You may well ask for fountains of rain
But that would be the worst thing you could gain.
For in the face of rain or of flood
Your mills must stand still, they can do no good.
But when the wind to a tempest will blow
Our mills work fast and clap to and fro.
According to the speed the wind can dictate
We adjust our sails to the very same rate.
Since our mills grind so much faster than yours
And since they may work at all times and hours,
I say we need no watermills at all
For windmills are sufficient to serve all.

WATER-MILLER: Though better than ours your mills grind faster
What use is this to those far away, good master,
In valleys and plains where all business is
There dwell most people – you grant me this?
On hills and downs which are most barren
There are few people; few can they sustain.
I dare even say you will find just now
That there are ten of us to one of you.
And where should all necessities be
But where people themselves are in plenty?
If rain falls reasonably as I require it
We shall not need of your windmills one little bit!

MERRY-REPORT *suddenly comes in through the audience.*

MERRY-R: Stop this, you fools, your reasoning is such
That you have reasoned too far and too much!
I heard all the words that you two have said.

Jupiter help me, you are both wrong in the head.
Neither of you has the wit nor the grace
That both mills will do in one place.
This I can tell from my own experience
For I have of my own, not far from hence
Standing together, a couple of mills,
Near to a marsh and between two hills.
The one for wind and the other for water.

He acts this with considerable zest.

My mills, in fact, are idle never.
For in a good hour, now take this to heart,
The water gates are no sooner apart
But clap, says the windmill, just behind
And there is good speed and both of them grind.
But whether the hopper is dusty
Or my millstones are somewhat rusty,
By the mass, the meal is horribly musty
And if you think my tale is not trusty
I make you this promise: come wind or rain
And you shall sample my grain.
So, as you hear, they lack neither wind nor water,
And as you have told and quarrelled on this matter

He extends arms to them both.

No more do yours as your needs do require,
But since you cannot agree I will desire
Jupiter to set both your minds at rest
About your wealth his honour will know best.

WATER-MILLER: I earnestly hope you will remember me.
WIND-MILLER: Let me not be forgotten, I beg of ye.

The two MILLERS, *pausing to address the final lines to Merry-Report leave the stage together quarrelling anew. During the following line the* GENTLEWOMAN *enters (stage left) and makes her way towards the audience.*

MERRY-R: Now we are rid of two rogues at one go!
GENTLEWOMAN: Goodness, what folly is this?

So many people. What can be amiss?
Sir, to you I have some little matter:
My coming is to speak with Lord Jupiter.

MERRY-R (*skittish again in the presence of a woman*):
Stand still a while and I will find out
Whether the god will hear you or not.

He approaches Jupiter's throne.

My lord, look here! Look up merrily!
A darling is here, by St Anthony.
Here has come to you a young treasure
Who would speak with you a measure.
If it be your pleasure to marry,
Speak quickly, for she may not tarry.

JUPITER: Silence! Why comes she to my court?
Hear out her reason, then return to report.

MERRY-REPORT *returns to the Gentlewoman at the front of the stage.*

MERRY-R: Mistress, you cannot speak with the god.

GENTLEWOMAN: No! why?

MERRY-R: By my faith, his lordship is so busy
With a piece of work that has to be done:
Even now he is making a fair new moon.
But tell me your business, then go away;
I will think about it when you are on your way.

GENTLEWOMAN: In truth, why I come here is this:
I am a woman quite fair, as you see;
No creature is more beautiful than me.
And since I am fair, fair would I stay.
No part of the year I know where to turn me
So back in my home am I forced to hide me.
The sun in summer so sorely does burn me
And in winter the wind on all sides would turn me.
I come to crave this for all women's sake
To send us weather close and temperate.
No sunshine, no frost, nor any wind to blow
Then could we set our beauties on show.

MERRY-R: Strut where you will; I swear by St Quintine
    You beat them all in your view and mine.
GENTLEWOMAN: If we only had weather to walk at our leisure
    Our lives would be merry beyond all measure:
    One part of the day spent in dressing,
    Another part for eating and drinking,
    And all the rest in the streets for walking
    Or in the house spending time in talking.
The LAUNDRESS *comes suddenly upon the scene (stage right).*
LAUNDRESS: Why! you here already. Then we are well met,
    For your demands contrary to mine are set.
    But I trust the god will be so indifferent
    That she will not receive what is in her intent.
As the two women take up positions for a heated discussion, MERRY-
REPORT *stands between them.*
MERRY-R: No doubt he will deal so graciously
    That everyone will be served impartially.
    I am telling the truth, for my office is such
    That I must report each suit – little or much.
LAUNDRESS: I fear that she wants to banish the sun.
    If so, we poor laundresses are quite done.
    Unless the sun shines for our clothes to dry
    We can do nothing in our laundry.
    What is worse is that we should lose
    To such a flirt as this wanton goose.
GENTLEWOMAN: I would rather that you should envy me,
    Than I should receive false pity.
    Because it is beyond you to be beautiful
    You think that we who are fair are disdainful.
LAUNDRESS: When I was as young as you are now
    I was quite as fair as you are now,
    As fair and pretty as any one of you all,
    But I was afraid of perils to fall.
    So with a business I did myself provide
    In case vice should draw me aside

As it quickly can where idleness has rein.
It is not your beauty that I disdain,
But your idle life which you have preserved
Which no good woman's heart could have loved.
For I see that in dancing and singing,
In eating and drinking and always dressing
All your heart and mind are set.
But none of this did your own labour get.
It seems to me you should leave such idleness
And spend more time in some honest business.
All women must be idle for you to have
The bright sun banished, as now you crave.
For out of the two I think it far better
Your face to be sunburnt and your clothes the sweeter,
Than that the sun from shining be smitten
To keep your face fair and all your clothes rotten.

MERRY-R: Get you both gone, I ask you sincerely.
I hear your suits and will report them truly.

GENTLEWOMAN: Sir, if you can, remember me first.
She leaves the stage to the right.

LAUNDRESS: Then how can I get anything but the worst?
She leaves in the opposite direction more dejectedly.

MERRY-R: Is not this a happy task that I have
For every drab to think me a knave?
Nobody knows what god's service is;
I myself never knew before this.
I think god's servants may live holily
But the devil's for sure live merrily.

As he saunters back towards the throne the BOY *picks his way through the audience, looking lost.*

BOY (*brightening*): This must be here in all likelihood.
Sir, I pray you, are you not master god?

MERRY-R: No, indeed I am not, but indeed I am he
The great good lord Jupiter acknowledges me.
If by the god you want anything done,

Tell me your wants and I will tell him, son.

BOY: Well, sir, my mind is this, in a few words:
All my pleasure is in catching birds,
And in making snowballs and throwing the same.
So on my way here a plan I did frame
To beg for great frost for my cunning pitfalls
And plenty of snow to make my fill of snowballs.
This done, boys' lives would be such as no man leads.
Oh, to see my snowballs land on my friends' heads.
And to hear the birds, how they flutter their wings
Deep in my pitfall. That passes all things!
Sir, if you are god's servant or kinsman
I beg you to help me in this if you can.

MERRY-R: Poor boy; who sent you hither?

BOY: A hundred boys were standing together
When they heard someone in the town cry
That my godfather, god almighty,
Had come from heaven of his own accord
This night to dine in this town with my lord.
And, further, he said come up who will
They should indeed have their belly made full,
Of all the weathers that they would ever crave,
And that is the weather that they might have.

And when my friends thought that this could be had,
And know that I am always a chattering lad,
They agreed after a great noise,
'Send little Dick,' cried all the boys.
I am here and beg you now as thus:
Help and implore the god to give it us.
And if of his weather god will give none,
I pray you, will he sell some?
Or lend us a bushel of snow, or twain,
And tell us how we may repay him again?

MERRY-R: I do not know (*puzzled for the first time*) I cannot tell;

I have not borrowed any from him at all.
But by such inquiries as I shall make
You will soon see what course he will take.
BOY: Sir, I thank you. Then I may depart?
The BOY *begins to take his way through the audience much more happily.* MERRY-REPORT *is now left to work out the different demands and is at a loss.*
MERRY-R: Farewell, good son, with all my heart. (*Pause*)
Now, such a crowd as here has been
In all my life I have never seen.
No suitors these, but women, fools and boys
And all their suits but fancies and toys!
If no one wiser comes after this cry
I will to the god and make an end quickly.
He addresses his request for the last time to the assembled audience.
Oyez! Oyez! if any person here
Be willing to appear,
For weather foul or clear,
Come on before this flock;
And be he whole or sickly
Let him show his mind quickly.
And may his tale be likely! Oyez! Oyez!
Having walked up and down, he pauses. Nobody comes forward.
All this time, I see, is put to waste
In waiting for suitors. I see none make haste.
Therefore I will tell the god this process
And be relieved of my humble office.
He goes to the throne of Jupiter.
Now lord, according to your commandment,
In hearing suitors I have been diligent,
And, as at first your will was I should
I come at last to say what each man would.
He ticks them off on his fingers.
Your first man wanted weather clear and not windy;
The second the same *and* breezes to blow sweetly.

The third desired storms and wind most extremely.
The fourth only water and would have no wind.
The fifth no water, but all wind to grind.
The sixth would have none of these, nor any bright sun,
The seventh dearly the hot sun would have won,
While the eighth and last for frost and snow he prayed:
These are the requests that all eight have made.

The number is small – here are two less than ten –
And yet, I fear, among ten thousand men
Nothing could stand any further from the other!
Not one of their suits agrees with another.
If you ask me, all this is great folly;
It is all beyond me, in the name of god's body.

JUPITER: Son, you have been diligent and done so well,
That your labour is now all praiseworthy.
But be sure I need no piece of your counsel.
For long since I have foreseen the remedy
Which you shall see. Go fetch all the suitors here
And command them all before us to appear.

MERRY-REPORT *acknowledges the command with a slight bow and goes out (stage left) to find his eight suitors.*

Of the struggle in heaven you have heard
Of the debate on earth among yourself you see.
As long as tempers of men are so frayed
So long will everyone live afraid.
This you can see, but no one can help but I.

MERRY-REPORT *leads back the chattering suitors.*

MERRY-R: How I have sought them
To bring them with me.
Yet have I brought them
Such as they be!

The GENTLEMAN, *obviously at his ease, silences the quarrelling group and steps forward to speak.*

GENTLEMAN: May it please your majesty, thus it is:

We as your subjects and humble suitors all,
According to that which your pleasure is,
Have sped to your presence, being principal
Head and king of all in every place.
Therefore we all commit ourselves to your grace.
JUPITER: As long as discretion so well may guide
So long shall I for your safety provide.
I have heard your griefs as you see,
To receive answer according to your degree.
And first to be told, most reason there is
The first man who sued: therefore mark this.

JUPITER motions the Gentleman to step out of the group and stand at the foot of his throne.

Often you will have weather clear and still
To hunt in for the recompense of your pain.

JUPITER gestures to the Merchant to follow. The GENTLEMAN *stands slightly to one side.*

And you merchants shall have your will,
For although no wind on land may remain
Yet on the sea pleasant breezes you shall obtain.

To the Gentleman and Merchant jointly.

And since your hunting must stop for the night,
The wind shall rise then, before the daylight.

The first suitors stand on the right while JUPITER *speaks next to the Ranger.*

The wind shall rattle down the wood in such a way
That all you rangers will have a good day.

The Ranger is dismissed and the two MILLERS *come forward together.*

And you water-millers shall have rains in the valley,
While at the same time on the hills I shall convey
Fair weather for windmills with such gusts of wind
That at one time both kinds of mills may grind.

The MILLERS *stand aside and the two women approach.*

And you fair women that close weather would have
I shall see to it – you may sufficiently

Have time to walk *and* save your beauty.
And yet shall those who live by laundry
Have hot sun enough your clothes to dry.

The women step into the line and the BOY *comes expectantly for his verdict.*

And you, pretty child, shall have both frost and snow.
So mark this conclusion, all you in this row.
Much better have I arranged for you all
That you all can perceive or could desire.
Each of you sued to have continual
Weather such as only his craft did require.
But I must serve the whole world and attend
To each sort of weather. Whatever may fall
Now one, now another, as I am pleased to send
Use it well and be assured that we shall
So guide the weather in course to each one of all.
That you may help each other to remain
In health and plentiful wealth certain.

Each suitor now steps forward again and speaks.

GENTLEMAN: Your grace has given to us here all in a row
And has expressed his will so bountifully
That I accept the word you are pleased to bestow
And thank you as the lord of all chivalry.

MERCHANT: Likewise, we merchants shall praise all wholly
The great name of god Jupiter,
As god of all gods, power solely,
For of everything, I see, you are nourisher.

RANGER: We shall give you our hearts with one accord
Since we know you as one only lord.

WATER-MILLER: What more can I do, but for your water
Give to your lordship Our Lady's Psalter.

WIND-MILLER: We are much in your debt, as I hope to be
saved,
We have obtained more than we craved.

GENTLEWOMAN: That is true. Your grace shall truly

Have the hearts of such as I, surely.

LAUNDRESS: And of those such as I (*to Gentlewoman*) who are as good as you.

BOY: Godfather god, I promise, if any snow come,

When I make my snowballs you shall have some.

The suitors form once more into a group and MERRY-REPORT *addresses the audience, laughing.*

MERRY-R: God thank your lordship. See how this is brought to pass.

Now we shall have weather just as ever it was.

JUPITER (*rises triumphantly*): My deeds declare who I am most potently

Both here on earth and in heavenly company.

My prudence has made peace universally.

This, I say, proclaims me principal

God and governor of heaven, earth and all.

Now, to that heaven, I shall make return

Where I am glorified most triumphantly.

Steps down from his throne and walks forward to the audience.

And you all, knowing me as your lord only

Rejoice in me most joyfully.

He passes through the audience and all the rest of the company follows.

THE END

THE PARDONER AND THE FRIAR

CHARACTERS

THE PARDONER

THE FRIAR

THE PARSON

CONSTABLE PRATT

SCENE: the nave of a church, perhaps suggested by a pulpit on one side, or signs of an altar-piece, or a backdrop of a stained-glass window. Entrances left and right and stage front, through auditorium.

THE PARDONER AND THE FRIAR

The play of *The Pardoner and the Friar* deals with two characters who were familiar to the Tudor audiences. The Pardoner also appears in the next Heywood play, *The Four P's*. In each of these plays we have more of a debate than a play with a significant plot. The interest and the comedy comes therefore from the argument between the Pardoner and the Friar. The object of that argument is to decide who is better able to save the souls of sinners. Of course, the sinners are conveniently played by the audience.

The Friar's first task – as he himself sees it at the opening of the play – is to convince the audience or 'congregation' that he is worth listening to. It was the Friar's job to do just this – to travel the countryside teaching and preaching. He was not supposed to have any possessions, nor should he desire any, but he had to live from day to day by begging. Our Friar declares that he has not come for 'meat nor for meal'. He has not come for money either, he says. It was the habit of Friars to collect money which was to be used to build churches or friaries, but often a large part of it was pocketed by the collector. The Friar says that he will pray first that his teaching will be effective and that his listeners will take note of the Word of God as he preaches it. The Friar takes up as his text a subject near to his heart: he deliberately mistranslates his Latin text 'Date et dabitur vobis' (Give, and it shall be given unto you) into 'Divide your goods the poor folk among'. Unfortunately (or fortunately?), the Friar is not allowed to get to the natural end of his preaching – the extracting of alms from his listeners.

But before the Friar can even begin his sermon, and whilst he is still praying, the Pardoner sidles on to the stage, loaded down with relics. The Pardoner has no less an unsavoury history than the Friar. Each is as unscrupulous as the other and both have the gift of the gab. The only difference is that the Pardoner is a little more transparent in his methods. The Friars were prepared to preach hellfire and damnation to extort money. The Pardoners were a little more underhand, for they sold 'pardons' which would protect from hellfire whoever bought or 'paid reverence to them'. As the Pardoner says later on in the play (see p. 50), once the Friar has preached the straight and narrow path, he leaves it at that; he (the Friar) does not care whether people get to heaven or not. The Pardoner, on the other hand, offers 'pardons' or 'indulgences', blessed by the Pope, which are virtually tickets straight to heaven. They confer on the buyer complete absolution from his sins in the after life so that there is no doubt that he should go to heaven.

It might be said that the Friar looked after this life and the Pardoner looked after the next one. But the Pardoner has a host of 'relics' which can take care of a number of present ailments. A 'relic' was, and is, some part of the anatomy of a saint, or a piece of his (or her) clothing, or some object connected with his life. When we realize that there are over 2,000 saints in the Catholic calendar, it is clear that there can be little shortage of the hips, arms, jaws, brains, mittens and veils that the Pardoner produces. Relics survive in their thousands today in Europe and are still widely venerated by Catholics who believe that by touching or praying *through* a relic, you become more pleasing to God. But praying *to* a relic would be idolatry.

In the middle ages, and at the time of this play, (1529), the veneration of relics would seem to have been related to the practice of witchcraft. Witchcraft depends on 'sympathetic magic' – the idea that a part can influence the whole. This means that by casting a spell on a *part* of someone's clothing or on a strand of his hair, you can cast a spell on the *whole* of that person. This is the kind of superstitious (rather than religious) belief that the Pardoner relies on when he produces his relics: by praying to these bits of saints, the whole of the saint's power may be called on. When the Pardoner starts producing his relics he really becomes a quack doctor selling his medicines: a hip-bone that will cure diseases in animals; a mitten that will increase crops; the arm of St Sunday that confers safety in travel; a toe which prevents toothache, and so on.

Heywood has quite clearly drawn heavily on Chaucer's *Canterbury Tales* for the characterization of his own pardoner and friar. In particular, Heywood has taken a number of details (especially concerning relics) from the *Pardoner's Prologue*. Chaucer's Pardoner also produces a bone which will cure animals, but it is the shoulder-bone of a sheep belonging to a holy Jew and not the holy Jew's own hip-bone. Both Pardoners have mittens which can multiply grain for whoever wears them. Heywood makes his Pardoner emphasize his papal authority, just as Chaucer's does. Heywood's Pardoner uses all the techniques which Chaucer's Pardoner is so sure will work that he tells everybody of them; Chaucer lists the methods by which pardoners had people eating out of their hands; the Pardoner cultivates haughty speech; he shows his papal bulls (or documents) and seals; he speaks some words in Latin to give his speech weight; and he has a pile of ragged relics.

In Heywood's comedy, the Pardoner and the Friar come face to face and engage in a running battle for the audience's attention and money. Each positions himself squarely in the middle of his half of the stage, well to the front, and plies his wares. In performance, the actors must be fast on their cues and the pace must be varied according to whether they have a single line to speak, or a couplet or four lines or more. On the occasions when they have only a line each at a time, they must be fired rapidly and confidently across the stage.

The Parson's intervention is timely. The third line that the Parson speaks – 'For polluting my church, a mischief on you light' – establishes from the beginning that the Friar and the Pardoner are speaking to a congregation in a church. A later line – 'No more of this wrangling in my church' – supports this idea. If this *is* the setting, then the Parson's horror at the unseemly fighting going on when he comes on the stage is more understandable. What little we see of the Parson suggests that he is the least corrupted of our three churchmen here; certainly he cannot take care of himself when faced with two customers like the Pardoner and the Friar.

This interlude will be most effective in performance (no less than in reading), if it is remembered that a very intimate relationship was established between characters and audience originally. Entrances through the audience are therefore important since they help to bring the audience into the play. The Pardoner can do this even more by speaking as he is walking along, before he reaches the stage. Both the main characters are, of course, fighting for attention and so the convention is obvious. Actors should not be afraid of going right up to the edge of the stage and looking the audience straight in the eye when they speak. The Friar may be played as somewhat aged and retiring but nevertheless sly and hypocritical. The Pardoner is a little more brash and worldly-wise and travelled. When the plays were originally performed, the actors were dressed in the same kind of clothes as the spectators, so that the moral of the play would seem significant still. It might prove expedient, if period costumes are difficult to obtain, to perform this play in modern dress. The Friar and the Pardoner would be some minor members of the clergy, the Parson would be wearing a clerical collar, and the Constable would be dressed as a policeman. All manner of ingenuity may be used to make relics. A fairly racy and confident performance should prove a great success.

Enter the FRIAR, *a little cautiously, carrying a decorated bag. Advances to stage front and confidentially addresses the audience.*

FRIAR: God be with you; the Holy Trinity
   Preserve all that now here be!
   Dear brethren, if you will consider
   The reason why I have come hither,
   You would be glad to know my intent:
   I do not come here for money nor for rent,
   I do not come for meat nor for meal,
   But I come here for your soul's heal.
Begins to search in his bag.
   I do not come here to fable or to lie,
   But I come here your souls to edify.
   For we friars are bound the people to teach;
   The Gospel of Christ openly to preach,
   As did the apostles – by Christ their master sent,
   To turn the people and make them repent.
Finally extracts a heavy, bound book.
   But since the apostles from heaven would not come,
   We friars now must occupy their room.
   We friars have professed wilful poverty:
   In our purse we may have no penny.
   We may have no manner of care, nor think
   We for our meat or for our drink,
   But let our thoughts from such things be as free
   As be the birds that in the air flee.
Points to page at which he has opened book.
   Wherefore, my friends, to this text take heed:
   Beware how you despise the poor friars.
   Who in this world are Christ's ministers,
   But do them with a hearty cheer receive –

Lest your houses unblessed they happen to leave.
For then God will take vengeance in His ire.

Wherefore I then, that am a poor friar,
Did inquire where any people were
Who were disposed the Word of God to hear.
As I came here one did me tell
That in this town right good people did dwell,
Therefore I require all you that are present
To attend and give me due audience.

Looks around him.

But first of all,
Now here I shall
To God my prayer make,
To give you grace
All in this place
His doctrine to take.

*Turns partly away from the audience, kneels and begins to pray.
Meanwhile the* PARDONER *enters from the back of the auditorium,
speaking to the audience all the while.*

PARDONER: God and St Leonard send you all his grace –
As many as are assembled in this place!
Devout Christian people, here as you sit,
I have come here you to visit.
Wherefore let us pray thus – before I begin:
Our Saviour preserve you all from sin
And enable you to receive this blessed pardon,
(Which is the greatest under the sun):
Granted by the Pope in bulls sealed with lead.
He shall find pardon when he is dead
Who offers either groats or else pence
For these holy relics which, before I go hence,
I shall here show in open audience,
Exhorting you all to do them reverence.

Takes bone out of his bag.

First, I show you all now a holy Jew's hip –
A bone – I pray you; take good keep
Of my words, and mark them well.
If any of your beasts' bellies do swell,
Dip this bone in the water that it does take
Into its body, and the swelling shall slake.
And if any snake your beasts have stung,
Take this water and wash his tongue
And it shall be whole again. And, furthermore,
Of pox and scabs and every sore
It shall be quite whole that drinks of the well
That this bone is dipped in. It is the truth to tell.

Rummages in his bag and takes out a 'mitten'.

He that will put his hand in the mitten
Shall have great increase of the grain
That he has sown, be it wheat or oats –
But he must offer me pence or groats.

Takes out another bone.

And another holy relic you each see may:
The blessed arm of sweet Saint Sunday.
Whosoever is blessed with this right hand
Cannot go amiss at sea or on land.

Yet another bone is extracted from the bag.

And another holy relic here you may see:
The great toe of the Holy Trinity.
Whosoever in his mouth once does it take,
He shall never be diseased with toothache.

Produces a ragged piece of cloth.

Here is a relic of Our Lady full good:
Her veil which she wore with her French hood,
Whenever she went out, for sun-burning.
Women with child who are in mourning,
By virtue thereof shall soon be eased,
And of their pain also full soon released.
Here is another relic, a precious stone,

Produces another bone.

    Of All-Hallows the blessed jaw bone –
    A relic which never fails;
    Chiefly against poison it prevails.
    It preserves from poison every man!

Brings out spongy, dark object.

    Look at Saint Michael's very brain-pan,
    Which for headaches is a restorative
    For every man or beast that bears life.
    And it shall further stand him in better stead,
    For his head shall never ache when he is dead,
    But be as though he lay in a dead sleep.

    Therefore to these relics now crouch and creep,
    But see that you offering to them make,
    Otherwise no kind of profit can you take.
    And because you
    Shall unto me
    Give credence to the full,
    My authority
    You shall now see—
    Lo, here is the Pope's bull!

Produces and unrolls huge scroll with a large red seal and ribbons. Shows this gleefully to all the audience and then retires a little to rearrange his relics on the floor around him. The FRIAR *finishes praying, crosses himself, stands and moves to front-stage and begins his sermon, failing to notice the Pardoner.*

FRIAR: 'Date et dabitur vobis':
    This means in our English tongue,
    'Divide your goods the poor folk among'—

Pauses, as he turns the pages of his Bible. The PARDONER *turns, not noticing the Friar and begins on his patter.*

PARDONER: Worshipful masters, you will understand,
    Pope Leo the Tenth has granted with his hand
    And confirmed in bulls sealed with lead,

To all manner of people both alive and dead,
Ten thousand years and as many Lents of pardon,
When they die to go to Paradise Garden.

The FRIAR *realizes he has a rival for the audience's attention and raises his voice.*

FRIAR: Therefore give your alms in the largest wise;
Keep not your goods: fie, fie on the covetous!

PARDONER: Ay, by the mass, you cannot hear
For the babbling of yonder friar!

FRIAR: See the Scriptures. But I say, sirs, how
Tedious a babbling is coming from yonder fellow!

PARDONER: Even so, masters, as I was about to tell,
Pope Julius and many more popes as well
Have granted clean remission of your sin –
As long as you put in
Some money into my coffer,
Or any money up into it offer.

FRIAR: But I say, you Pardoner, I bid you hold your peace!

PARDONER: And I say, you Friar, make your tongue cease!

FRIAR: Why do you stand there all day chattering?

PARDONER: Indeed! and why do you stand there all day
    clattering?

FRIAR: Come, fellow, I am here to preach the Word of God,
In which task I cannot be forbidden.
For he who denies the Word of God a hearing
Stands accursed in the last reckoning.
You are sure accursed for interrupting me.

PARDONER: No, *you* are cursed – that you will see!
And to all that to me make interruption,
The Pope sends them excommunication.

Turns on the Friar.

And if you disturb me in anything,
You are also a traitor to the king.
For he has granted me here, under his royal seal,

Producing another large scroll and pointing to the seal.

That no man should disturb me in my appeal.
Goes up to Friar and thrusts his nose into Friar's face.
  You, Friar, once having taught the way,
  Do not care whether they *(pointing to audience)* come to heaven,
    yea or nay.
  And all that you can imagine
  Is how to use virtue – and abstain from sin.
  And if they once fall, *(again points to audience)* you can do no
    more:
  You cannot give them a cure for their sore.
Turns to audience and continues victoriously.
  But these letters are complete purgation,
  However many sins you may have done.
  For I shall bring you to heaven's gate
  And be your guide in another state –
  So that you shall not fall, as I told.
FRIAR: Hold your peace, knave, you are too bold:
  You prate, in faith, like a pardoner.
PARDONER: Why do you despise the Pope's minister?
To the audience.
  Masters, here I curse him openly,
  And thereby warn all this company
  By the Pope's authority,
  That you leave him and listen to me.
  Till he is absolved, his words have no effect,
  For out of the Holy Church he is quite reject.
FRIAR: My masters, he does but jest and rave;
  Do not believe the words of a knave.
  But to the Word of God do reverence,
  And hear me through with due deference.
  Masters, I told you just now of alms indeed,
  And how you should give to poor folk at their need—
PARDONER: —Masters, this pardon which I showed you before
  Is the greatest ever, since Christ Mary bore—
FRIAR: —And if you once that thing have done,

Doubt not that God will give you retribution—

PARDONER: How else, without confession or contrition
But by this shall you have complete remission?—

FRIAR: —But I hope, Pardoner, you will be silent soon!—

PARDONER: —Yes; it is likely to be when I have done!—

FRIAR: —But I say, you rude fellow, you,
Was there no other time for your bulls but now?

PARDONER: I *will* read them now: what say you then?
Have you anything to do with them?

FRIAR: Well, *I* will begin, and then let me see,
Whether you will dare again interrupt me.
To go on from where I left off just now,
Our Lord in the Gospel shows the way how—

The PARDONER *interrupts again.*

PARDONER: Because some will perhaps think wrong of me,
You will now hear the Pope's authority—

First the FRIAR, *then the* PARDONER *loses his temper.*

FRIAR: By God's word, knave, I'll suffer you no longer—

PARDONER: I say somebody, (*to audience*), lend me a hammer
And I'll make that bald crown of his look red!
I shall leave him but one ear on his head!

FRIAR: But I shall not leave you one ear before I go—

PARDONER: Oh! wretched Friar, will you so?

They set to and fight.

FRIAR: Loose your hands away from my ears—

PARDONER: Then take your hands away from my hairs—

FRIAR: Yes, but will you still bite and scratch?

PARDONER: Yes indeed I will, as long as you thrash.

Enter the PARSON.

PARSON: Hold your hands; a vengeance on you two
That you ever came here to make this to-do!

The PARDONER *and the* FRIAR *hurriedly disentangle themselves.*

I swear to you by God's holy might,
You will both repent, every vein of your heart,
As sore as you ever did, before you depart.

The FRIAR *takes the* PARSON *aside.*

FRIAR: Master Parson, I marvel that you will give licence
    To this false knave, in this audience
    To publish his ragman-rolls with lies.
    I desired him, he knows, more than twice
    To hold his peace until I had done;
    But he would hear no more than the man in the moon—

The PARDONER *has been listening and interrupts.*

PARDONER: Why should I suffer *you* more than you *me*?
    Master Parson gave the licence, as you see.
    I would you knew, I have relics here
    And all manner of stuff you do not share.

He seizes his chance and begins to preach again.

    I will edify more with the sight of it
    Than will all your prating of holy writ—

PARSON: No more of this wrangling in my church!
    I blame you both for this lurch.
    Is there any bloodshed between these knaves?
    God be praised they had no staves
    Nor blades, for it would have been wrong.
    Well, I will make you sing another song!

Looks over the audience's heads.

    Constable Pratt, come here, I you pray!

Enter CONSTABLE PRATT *through the audience. He notices the*
PARDONER *and the* FRIAR *brushing their clothes.*

CONSTABLE: Why, what is all this nice fray?

PARSON: I cannot say: this knave disdains the other;
    Therefore you take the one, and I shall the other.
    We shall stow them where it is most convenient.
    I promise that this couple shall repent
    That they ever met in this church here.
    As you are the constable, you stand near.
    You take that tall knave, and let me alone
    With this gentleman; by God and Saint John,
    My fist will soon itch and take me too far.

CONSTABLE: You may well do that: they must learn to beware.

PARDONER: Master Pratt, I am sorry for what I have done.
Therefore I pray you to forgive me soon;
I will never come here more,
While I live, God before.

CONSTABLE: No. I am charged with your custody,
And so, by Saint John, you will not escape me
Till you have filled a pair of stocks.

PARSON: In all his pleading he only mocks!

Begins to take FRIAR *out, off stage, by the arm.*

PARDONER: No, Master Parson, for God's passion,
Do not treat me after that fashion:
It does not suit your honesty.

PARSON: Honesty or not, but you shall see
What I shall do by and by:
Do not struggle, come along soberly:
For it will not avail you I say.

FRIAR: Indeed? – that we shall test straightaway.
I defy you, as long as there is only you.
I will not go with you, I make God a vow.
We shall first see who is the stronger:
God has sent me bones; you I do not fear.

Breaks free from the Parson and stands his ground.

PARSON (*undaunted*): Constable Pratt, bring forward that knave.
And you, sir friar, will you always rave?

FRIAR: Yes, fool, I you defy!
I shall trouble you first.
'You will go to prison by and by.'
Humph! Let me see you now do your worst!

CONSTABLE PRATT *struggles with the* PARDONER, *the* PARSON
with the FRIAR. *The* PARSON *is soon in trouble with the wily* FRIAR.

PARSON: Help! help! Constable Pratt, Constable Pratt.
In the good name of God, help me somewhat!

CONSTABLE (*panting*): No. Deal as you can with that elf,
For I have enough to do myself.

Alas! for pain I am almost dead;

The red blood is running so down my head.

Rather, *if* you can, I pray you help me.

PARSON: No, by the mass, fellow, it cannot be.

I have more weight against me than I can twin;

The cursed friar does the upper hand win.

By this time both the PARSON *and the* CONSTABLE *are on their knees.*

FRIAR: Will you stop then, and let us in peace depart?

PARSON and CONSTABLE: Yes, by Our Lady, even with all my heart.

FRIAR and PARDONER: Then adieu; to the devil; till we come again!

Exit both, through the audience, having picked up their belongings.

PARSON and CONSTABLE: And a mischief go with you both twain!

They are left to pick themselves up wearily and stagger off stage.

THE FOUR P'S

CHARACTERS

A PALMER

A PARDONER

A POTHECARY

A PEDLAR

SCENE: an open space. Entrances right and left and centre.

THE FOUR P's

The original title of this Interlude was *Four PP* in which the doubled capital letter stood for the plural form; in the same way, the abbreviation *pp.* is used today as short for 'pages'. It was a clever stroke of the writer John Heywood to combine a group of people by the initial letters of their professions, especially when it is realized that in their own day these four occupations were always thought to breed liars.

There is no real plot, but a debate upon the reliability of each person in the group. Towards its close the Interlude almost becomes a Morality play designed to teach the need for sincerity. Having seen a group of such liars, the thought runs, we should value truth the more highly.

Palmer is the first to arrive, an old man who has spent his whole life wandering round the world visiting saints' tombs and places housing holy objects – all for the good of his soul. Clearly a sincere person, he is also too ready to believe the pious stories that have been told. The Pardoner comes across him, making a second appearance in a Heywood play, repeating some of his earlier lines and bringing out some of his old relics. We have already commented upon him on p. 42.

Pedlar represents the salesman travelling round from door-to-door or standing upon a village green offering rubbish, while Pothecary (or Apothecary) is a chemist who is also a quack-doctor and therefore immediately a suspicious character.

The first point under discussion is whether Palmer or Pardoner has the more certain way to heaven: by pilgrimages or by pardoning. The Pothecary is a more earthy type and points out that there is nothing like a course of medical treatment to drive a man either to heaven or to hell. The Pedlar makes no high claims for his wares apart from the subject of life and death, and he offers to stand back and judge which of the other contestants is the best. There is no prize. Only in the field of lying can they possibly compete and finally they all agree to tell one glorious lie each.

Pothecary and Pardoner make strenuous attempts to try and win. The reader may decide which of these lies he thinks the most outrageous. The fate of the medical swab that did so much damage is perhaps the most inventive, but the description of the devils in hell is superior for sheer witty poetry. A sneeze (which still invokes the statement 'bless you' in this country) has a comic outcome for the soul who is released from purgatory. The winning lie that sweeps the other contestants off their feet is the simplest of all. Palmer boldly states that he has never found an impatient woman.

Even then the issue is not clear, because the losers are unhappy at the verdict. Therefore the Pedlar has to sum up that nobody has really lost or won because each has much to be said on his behalf. The verdict is understood when the closing sermon is studied: If you have good motives behind what you do you are in no danger of doing wrong. The verdict on Pothecary is that he is a truthful man and therefore also on the first steps to goodness and grace.

In performance there is need to distinguish the voices and bearing of the four contestants as far as possible. During the long speeches that are essential to story-telling, the players should not attempt to distract the audience by too much stage business, but rather listen and respond to the speaker. The Pedlar and the Pardoner should each have packs but the latter is intended to look greyer and more churchy and unpleasant than the former. He might have a hood with a vernicle sewn upon it. Pothecary must carry some bottles of physic with him. Palmer should sport a large stick and the kind of lapel badge which was given to every pilgrim on a pilgrimage until their collection might well have resembled those found on modern cars. The stage can be bare apart from some form of seating. A specific location for the action is not important, and whilst the idea of the remote past is retained, it is not difficult to bring out the current value of the moral.

Enter PALMER *with a staff and a palm leaf in his hand, signifying his role in the play. He comes from one side and advances to the front of the stage, speaking in a manner that is both simple and pompous in turn. He is elderly and slow-moving.*

PALM: I am a palmer, as you may see,
  And of my life much have I spent
  In many a fair and far country
  As pilgrims do with good intent.

He begins to enumerate place-names on his fingers.

  To Jerusalem have I been
  Before Christ's most sacred shrine.
  The Mount of Calvary have I seen,
  The end it marked of His earthly design.
  To Jehosophat and Mount Olivet,
  On foot, God knows, that foot all bare.
  Many a salt tear did I sweat
  Before this body could ever get there.
  And I have been to Rome also
  To pilgrimage-stations all in a row,
  St Peter's shrine and many more to know.
  On the hills of Armenia there I saw Noah's ark;
  To the home of Job, to St George in Southwark.
  To Wales to St David and to France to St Denys,
  To St Matthew and St Mark in Venice.
  To these and many another one[1]
  Devoutly I have prayed and gone.

The PARDONER *with his package stuffed full of papal bulls and pardons enters behind his back from the opposite corner. He listens to the end of the speech and then advances.*

PALM: Imploring them to pray for me
  Unto the Blessed Trinity.

[1] Local place names could well be inserted in rhyme.

The PARDONER *shows that he is a more professional speaker; he is
more glib and not in the slightest hesitant.*

PARD: And so, you have gone as far as you can
    For all your labour and holy intent.
    You're welcome home as wise as you went.

PALM: Why, sir, despise a pilgrimage?

PARD: No, no, good sir, be you not in a rage.
    I think you were well occupied
    Seeking out saints on every side.
    But, pray, show what the cause is
    You went on all these pilgrimages?

PALM: Forsooth, this life I did begin
    To rid me of all the bondage of sin.
    Beseeching saints to keep the record
    Of all my struggles before the Lord
    That grants man remission
    According to his state of contrition.

The PARDONER *at once sees that he has an audience and begins to
undo his package.*

PARD: Why go so far with help so nigh?
    When here at home is your remedy.
    Here at your door myself I do dwell
    Who could have saved your soul as well
    As all your world wandering could do
    Though you went thrice to Jericho.
    Now since you might have done well to stay at home
    What have you gained by gadding to Rome?

PALM: Tell me first what man you are.

PARD: Truly, I am a Pardoner.

PALM: Oh, seldom is it seen, or never,
    That truth and pardoners dwell together.
    I went myself to the very thing
    In every place, and no feigning.
    I had as much pardon there, assuredly,
    As you can promise here so doubtfully.

And of my labours I nothing repent,
For God will respect how each day is spent;
And since in His knowledge all is regarded,
So by His goodness all is rewarded.

He begins to start away from the Pardoner in a huffy temper. The
PARDONER *follows him.*

PARD: By the first part of your old tale
It seems you come but late from some ale.
Where you esteem your travels so much
I say yet again that my pardons are such
That if there were a thousand souls in a heap,
I would bring them to heaven all cheap.
At small cost and without any pain,
My pardons will lift them to heaven quite plain.

The POTHECARY *with a pack of medical goods enters from behind
the two. He speaks with the confidence of a market-trader.*

PARD: Give me a penny, or two pence
And as soon as your soul has departed hence –
In half an hour – or three quarters at most,
The soul is in heaven with the Holy Ghost.

POTH (*advances towards them*): So busy you are for your souls'
   health
May not a Pothecary come in by stealth?
And by the leave of this fair company,
Prove you knaves both before we go,
At least as smart talkers whose 'yes' is 'no'?
(*To Palmer*) You by hard work think heaven to get
(*To Pardoner*) All your trust upon pardons is set.
Now, no soul, you know, enters heaven's gate
Till from the body it is separate.
And whom have you known die honestly
Without the aid of an apothecary?
All that come into our handling
Unless one chance to end in a hanging –
That no way perhaps he shall have no need

Of a purge or glister to end, indeed.
Since of our souls a multitude
I send to heaven, when all is viewed,
Who but I should be thanked altogether
For sending them for their reward thither?

PARD (*growing irritated*): If you killed a thousand in one hour's
    space,
How get they to heaven in the right state of grace?

POTH: If a thousand pardons round each neck were tied,
How get they to heaven if they never died?

PALM: Long life full of good works, indeed.
Does hinder our reaching a heavenly meed.

*The PEDLAR with a pack of odds and ends enters from another corner
of the stage. He listens quietly.*

PALM: But death before our duty is done
Will make us think we have died too soon.

POTH (*seeing the newcomer*): Now, on my faith, full well matched
Where the devil were we four hatched?
You are a Palmer, and you are a Pardoner,
I am a Pothecary. What are you?

PED: I am a Pedlar.
Do you not know that every pedlar
In every trifle must be a great meddler?
Especially in women's triflings,
These seek we out above all other things.

Opens his pack and shows his goods.

This gear shows itself in such beauty
That everyone thinks it says, 'Come buy me!'
Look, you yourself can be the chooser,
You can name the price, though I be the loser.
Is there nothing for good father Palmer?
Have you no young lady in a quiet corner
For all your walking to the holiest places?
I have heard, I vow, of such strange cases.
Here you find many a good love token

Of which only a part may here be spoken.
Gloves, pins, combs, glasses unspotted,
Pomanders, hooks and laces knotted.

He brings different items out of his pack.

Brooches, rings and all manner of beads,
Laces round and flat for women's heads.
Needles, thread, thimbles, shears and knick-knacks:
Where lovers be such thing never lacks.

POTH: Do women buy their pincases of you?

PED: Yes, that they do, I make God a vow.

POTH: You people make her pincases so wide;
The pins will fall out, they cannot bide.
Great pins she must have, one or other,
And if she lose one she will find another.
And then I find good cause to complain;
New pins for her pleasure and my pain.

PARD: Sir, you seem well versed in women's causes.
I pray you, tell me what causes this
That women, after their arising
Spend so long in their apparelling?

PED (*with various imitated actions*): Forsooth, women have so
    many 'lets'[1]
Frontlets, fillets, partlets and bracelets.
With these 'lets' and nets the delay is such
That speed is small though haste is much.

POTH: And there is one thing they cannot forbear,
The trimming and pinning of all their gear,

He takes a pin from the Pedlar and imitates actions.

Especially fiddling with the tail-pin.
And when they would seek to prick it in,
If it chance to double in the cloth
They become mad and swear a great oath.
Till it stands right they will not forsake it.

---

[1] Coverings.

Thus, though it may not, yet would they make it.
But be sure, they do but defer it
And where they would make it they often mar it.
But prick them and pin them as much as you will,
Yet they will for more pinning still.

PED: Let women's matters pass, and now mark mine:
Whatever their points be, their points are fine.
Therefore, if you are willing to buy,
Lay down your money, and come quickly.

PALM: No, by my troth, we are like friars:
We are all beggars and none of us buyers.

PED (*closing his pack*): Then, by the faith of my body,
I like full well our little company.
Away with this pack, for it is plain
I go not hence with any large gain.
I show my wares because that is my mind,
But I think I shall no profit find.
This likes me well, as I am alive.

PARD: Yet, so help me God, I still must strive.
Such strife this man did first begin (*pointing to Palmer*)
When we were set before you came in.

PALMER *and* PARDONER *resume their original places.*
On foot he goes from place to place,
A pilgrim, calling out for grace.
He hopes through those pains for penitence
To gain discharge of his conscience.
And as we were deep in contention
In came this fool (*pointing to Pothecary*) with his invention
Reviling us both, himself advancing,
That all the souls to heaven ascending
Are bound most of all to the pothecary
Because he helps most men to die.
Before which death, he says indeed,
No soul in heaven can have his meed.

PED: Why, do pothecaries kill good men?

POTH: By God, men say so now and then!
PED: I thought you would not have missed
   To remain a long age upon your list.
POTH: Yes, but it is full necessary
   To send at last for a pothecary,
   And when you feel your conscience ready
   I can send you to heaven quickly.
   Therefore, concerning this matter here
   Above these two I stand, quite clear.
   And you (*To Pedlar*) shall be the judge in this case
   Which of us three shall take the first place.

*At this point in the action there is only a simple rivalry between
Pardoner and Palmer as at the opening. The pair should retain their
original positions with their spectator and judge rather less at ease.*

PED: I neither will judge the best nor the worst,
   For, be you blessed or be you cursed,
   It does not become pedlars or proctors
   To claim the judgement of learned doctors.
   Each of you has somewhat to show
   How souls towards heaven through you do grow.
   Then if you can so well agree
   To continue together, all three,
   And you all submit to one will,
   Then that man's task I can aim to fulfil.
   (*To Palmer*) If you came to judge one man
   Who had travelled further than you can,
   At once, father Palmer, you would discharge
   Him of his sins, no matter how large.
   (*To Pardoner*) For all his sins that he had contrition
   Your pardons would absolve and give contrition.
   (*To Pothecary*) And then, Pothecary, you could say
   You would send him off to heaven right away.
POTHECARY *produces a large box of tablets.*
POTH: If he taste from this box at the hour of prime,
   By the mass, he is dead by evensong time!

My skill is such that I can right well
Send my friends to heaven and myself to hell.
See then if we three may agree as one
We may be a Trinity of lords under sun.
If we three may be as one
Then are we great lords each and every one,
But, for good order, in a word,
Two of us must defer to the third;
And unto that I do agree
While both of you here wait upon me!

PARD: No, no, good friend, that cannot be,
I am too good to wait on three.

PALM: By Our Lady, I would be loath
To wait on the better of you both.

PED (*pacifying them*): Now, now, I pray, mark what I say:
One of the three the two must obey;
And since you cannot agree with one voice
Who shall be head, there is no choice
But to devise some special thing
Wherein you are of equal cunning
And in that he who can do best
Will have the others at his behest.
I think I can find one mystery
In which you can all do equally,
And that is neither in selling nor buying,
But even in this: it is in lying!
For you three all lie as well
As our Father of Lies down in hell.

His hearers look like out breaking into violence again.

And though you heard me refuse to budge
When in greater matters asked to judge
Yet in lying I too have some skill
And if I be judge, I will
You may be sure, without flattery
For whom my conscience finds award mastery.

For him my judgement shall straight be found,
  Although thus I might forfeit a thousand pound.
PALM: As for lying, though I can do it,
  I am indeed most loath to go to it.
PED (*to Palmer*): You have no cause to fear; be bold,
  For you can tell lies all uncontrolled.
  (*To Pardoner*) And you in this have great advantage
  For lying is but your common usage.
  (*To Pothecary*) And you at lying must be good
  Since your whole craft stands firm on falsehood.

They each register their growing annoyance as they are singled out for attack.

  I beg you take care who shall begin
  For each of you may well hope to win.
  Now, speak up, all three, how do you find?
  Are you content to follow my mind?

They calm down, seeing that they can now hope to win in esteem from entering the contest.

PALM: Yes, by my troth, I am content.
PARD: And in good faith I too assent.
POTH: If I refused, I were a noddy,
  For this trick is mine, by God's body.

PARDONER *seizes a chance to show his wares but his audience is more critical. As he names each item he produces it from his pack and raises it for everybody to see.*

  Now, if riches can rule this roost,
  Behold what cause I have to boast.
  Look, here are pardons half a dozen,
  For spiritual riches they have no cousin.
  Still more, to me they bring
  Sufficient supplies for a good living.
  Here I have relics of such a kind
  As in this world no man can find.
  Kneel down, all three, and when you cease kissing,
  He who offers shall gain my blessing.

Friends, here shall you see anon
Of All-Hallows[1] the blessed jaw-bone.
POTH: Whew! by All-Hallows methinks
How foully All Hallows' breath now stinks!
PARD: Now, sirs, behold, here you may see
The great toe of the Holy Trinity.
Who to this toe any money here voweth
And once does roll it about in his mouth,
All his life after, I undertake,
He shall be rid of the pains of toothache,
POTH: I pray you, turn that relic about:
Either the Trinity had the gout
Or else, because it is three toes in one,
God made it large as three toes alone.
PARD: We let that pass, look now upon this.
Here is a relic that cannot miss
To help the least as well as the most.
I have here the buttock-bone of Pentecost.
Mark well this relic – a true outstripper –
My friends, 'tis true, here is a slipper
Of one of the Seven Sleepers, be sure.
Indeed one kiss shall bring you great pleasure.
For all of two days it shall so ease you
That no other saviours shall displease you.
POTH: All of two days! No, all of two year
For none of the savours that may come here
Can be any worse; why, now I'll be hung
One of the Sleepers trod in the dung.
PED: Sir, I think your devotion is very small.
PARD: Small, why, indeed, he has none at all.
POTH: What the devil care I what you think?
Shall I praise relics when they all stink?
PARD: Here is a box full of bumble-bees
That stung mother Eve as she sat on her knees,
[1] All Saints.

Tasting the fruit to her forbidden.
Who kisses the dead bees this box hidden
Shall have as much pardon, as of right
As for any relic he kisses this night.

PALM: Sir, I will kiss them, with all my heart.

POTH: Do, kiss them once more to add in my part
For I am not worth – I must let them be –
Those bees that stung Eve shall not sting me.

As he is unpacking more goods the POTHECARY produces some of his medicinal wares.

POTH: Have you not about you remains in a glass
Of the wine that at the wedding was
Of Adam and Eve? It must indeed be sour and stale,
So, for the Lord's sake, help me to cup of fresh ale.
Richer by far than all your tackle
Is this box though it do no miracle.
I hold a packet of rhubarb here
Which is as dainty as it is dear.
To the best friend I have on English ground
It is worth at the least a good twenty pound,
For though the stomach does this abhor
It purges you clean from your choler.
If you taste but one crumb and take it from me (*hands some
out*)
If you ever are hanged then never trust me.
Here I have *diapompholicus*,
A special ointment all doctors discuss:
For a fistula or for a canker
This is indeed a very sheet-anchor.
This is the syrup of *Byzansis*
Only a little is enough of this.
Then I have others: *diospoliticon*
Mercury sublime and *metridaticon*
Pellitory and *asafoetida*
Cassy and *colloquintida*.

These are the things that furnish the strife
Between man's sickness and the loss of his life.
From all your pains these shall you deliver
And set your mind well at rest for ever.
Such are the medicines with which I can
Help your beasts as well as a man.
(*To Pedlar*) Now I beg your vote fall to me,
And if any reward of use shall be,
Then shall you have my marmalade
So rich you may dig it out with a spade.
PED: Good sir, I thank you, but your reward
Is not the thing that I regard.
I have devised for this test another way
In which all three your minds you betray.
For each of you one tale now shall tell
And which of you contrives it so well
As most unlikely to be true
Then he shall prevail whatever ensue.
POTH: If you want some fine marvelling,
Then shall you hear a marvellous thing.
He advances to the centre of the stage to tell his lie.
I did a cure no longer ago
Than Anno Domini Millesimo[1]
On a young woman, so bright and so fair
That never have I seen anyone gayer.
Her head was so giddy and her heels so short
How oft she fell down I cannot report.
For in the twinkling of an eye
Down would she fall in the wet or the dry.
Before she would rise on her feet again
I used all my skill and took much pain,
But could not with ease bring her right round
Though I placed a great swab inside a deep wound.
Had she been my own youngest sister

[1] A.D. 1000.

I could not have devised so fine a glister.
I feared that the swab would be heavy to carry
And I was afraid it would never there tarry.
Suddenly as if it had thundered
It was out with a clap and a noise like a bombard.[1]
Now mark, for here starts the revel,
This swab flew ten miles along on the level
To a fine castle built of lime and stone –
For strength I knew not another such a one –
Which stood on a hill so high
At the foot of which a river ran by.
When this bung on the castle did sharply alight
It put the building so vastly to flight
That down the stones crashed, one on another,
No stone was left standing, by God's dear mother.
They rolled so fast right down the steep hill
In such a vast number that they it did fill
From bottom to brim, from shore to shore
That fast-flowing river, so deep before.
So was the girl relieved with such violence
Of all her pain and inconvenience.

PED: Sir, of the cure I can nothing tell,
But to our present purpose you have spoken well.

PEDLAR *and* POTHECARY *bow politely to each other and the latter
gives his place to the* PARDONER *who advances to tell his lie.*[2]

PARD: The cure which I intend you shall hear
Of a friend departed within seven year
Began when she sickened suddenly
And fell dead almost immediately.
When I thought how this had chanced,
And of all the souls I to heaven had advanced

[1] Large gun.
[2] In the original version this speech runs to 200 lines so that it cannot
be reduced too far. The purgatory passage at least could be cut in a
performance.

Though I could not guard my friend from the dangers,
As I had done to so many that were but strangers,
That was the thing that grieved me so;
Nothing on earth could release my woe.
To find out how her soul did stand
I took a long journey out of hand.
He acts his story, the vigour increasing all the time.
Now give ear to my wonderful story:
From here I went straight to purgatory.
I knocked and was let in quickly.
And, Lord, how low the souls made curtsey!
I asked them this question then
If such a soul from the world of men
Did late among them there appear.
Thereto they said she had come never there.
On this I chanced once to sneeze,
'Christ help!' called a soul that awaited his fees.
And with my pardons of all degree
I paid his toll and set him so free
That straight to heaven and off was he!
Alas, I thought, my friend is in hell.
I feared me much that all was not well.
So off to the devil that kept the gate
I called and spoke up after this rate:
'All hail, sir devil, good master porter—'
But, now to make this tale all the shorter,
'Help me', I said, 'to talk with your Lord and master.'
'Be sure', said he, 'no tongue can tell
What time you could have ever have come so well.
For this is the day that Lucifer fell
And so it is kept our Festival of Hell.
Nothing unreasonable craved on this day
Shall by him be met with a nay.'
The devils all stood, their claws full clean,
Their tails well combed, and I mean,

With slippery butter their bodies anointed.
I never saw devils so smartly appointed.
The master devil sat down there in his jacket,
While all the souls were playing at racket.
No rackets they had in claw or hand
Save that every soul held a fire-brand.
Lucifer smiled and laughed merrily
    And spoke to me well-favouredly,
Rolling his eyes, as round as two bushels,
Flashing the fire out of his nostrils.
'Be good to grant the thing I crave.'
I said in short, 'This would I have.
The soul of one who hither has flitted
Into these hands today remitted.'
'Now,' said the devil, 'we are well pleased.
What is his name you would have thus eased?'
'Nay,' said I, 'be it good or evil
My calling is but for a certain she-devil.'
'What do you call her?' – and he played with his hook.
'Forsooth,' I remarked, 'she is Margery Cook.'
'Now, by our honour,' said Lucifer,
'No devil in hell shall withhold her.
Apply all your pardons to women so
That unto us here no more come, no, no!'
    I was taken then into the kitchen,
For Margery's office lay all day therein,
Before her the meat was half-roasted indeed,
But I took her off the spits with great speed.
Oh, all the devils, for joy how they
Did roar aloud on that happy day.
And to conclude this long tale so briefly
The woman she thanked me chiefly.
If any man now thinks he would mind her
On Newmarket Heath is where he will find her.
The PARDONER *exhausted with telling his tale subsides.*

PED: Sir, you have told us all your wonders well
 And where you found your friend as you tell.
 To think that you went all the way to hell,
 That was indeed to come into great peril.
PALM: His tale is in every part most perilous
 But one thought I find quite marvellous.
 Where you said that all devils complain
 That women all cause them great pain.
 This, in fact, he told for truth
 And that to me is a marvel, forsooth.
 How women in hell such shrews can be
 Yet here so gentle must defeat poor me.
 For I have tramped many a mile
 Seen many a woman in all that while;
 I would have you all understand
 I have met no less than five hundred thousand.
Then rest of the group begins to look quite incredulous.
 In all the places where I have been
 And all the women that I have seen,
 I never met or knew, on my conscience,
 One single good woman out of her patience.
The others are ready to explode with disagreement.
POTH: By the mass, that is a huge great lie!
PARD: I never heard one greater, by Our Lady!
PED: One greater? Indeed, knew you ever one so great?
 Then shall my judgement be no more delayed.
 Of all these three, if each man's tale
 In Paul's Churchyard were put on sale
 From some man's pen that has the skill
 He would bring great sums into his till.
 (*To Pothecary*) Sir, all the tale that you did tell
 I bear in mind. (*To Pardoner*) And yours as well.
 As you saw your subjects discreetly
 You both lied well and neatly.
 Yet were your lies among the least, trust me.

For if you (*To Pothecary*) had said you had made flee
Ten swabs out of ten women for fee
Ten times ten miles to ten castle walls
To fill ten rivers, ten times burst walls.
Or if you (*To Pardoner*) ten times had bodily
Fetched ten souls from out of purgatory
And ten times as many out of hell,
Yet, by my ten finger bones I could right well
Ten times sooner every part believed
Than a mere tenth part of what we have received.
POTH: Ten times I beseech Him that on high sits
    Your wife's ten commandments may hurt your five wits.
    And twenty times ten this wish I would:
    That you had been hanged at ten years old.
    And here is another that would take my part.
PARD: Yes, and first I curse you black knavish heart.
    (*To Pedlar*) Sir, I beseech your worship to be
    As good as you can be unto me.
PED: I would be glad to do you some good,
    And him also, for I am in the right mood.
    Both your tales I judge as quite impossible
    But his I take to be yet more incredible.
    Not only the tale itself allows it
    But its very boldness plainly avows it.
He advances towards the audience.
    So, now, if you please to take my order
    Among all the women within this border
He points at individual women near-by.
    Take three of the youngest and three of the oldest,
    Three of the hottest and three of the coldest,
    Three of the fairest and three of the maddest,
    Three of the foulest and three of the saddest.
    When all these threes are parted asunder
    In each three, two at least in number,
    Shall be found frank shrews. Unless this should befall

That you should to find them shrews everyone all.
He himself (*pointing to Palmer*) all this does know
For well he knows some in this row,
And yet he swears by his conscience
That he never met a woman out of patience.
Of all the lies that this day have been spent
His lie is indeed the most excellent.

PARD (*To Pothecary furiously*): Marry, sir, we no less can do
Than thank him indeed for that judgement so true.
That will I do for my own part
With a dark vengeance on his knave's heart.
I never knew a pedlar be a judge before,
Nor will I trust peddling rogue any more.

The defeated candidates bow ironically to the Pedlar.

POTH: Courtesy before, and courtesy behind him,
A bow on each side, may the devil blind him!
It is not soon learned, dear peddling brother,
One knave to make courtesy to any other.

PARD: It then would be said, take me at my word,
Two knaves made courtesy to the third.

PED: Now are you all as you have begun,
No man has lost, no man has won.
By way of advice I will speak as I can.
(*To Palmer*) I do perceive that pilgrimage
Is the thing for which you show a badge,
And so do you in your pretence (*To Pardoner*)
That you can procure an indulgence
For all your neighbours charitably
For the love of each in God only.
Both of your walks come to one end
And so for all that do here pretend
By aid of God's grace to ensue
All manner and kind of holy virtue.
Some great alms are seen to give
Some in wilful poverty to live:

Some to make roads and such like works
Some to maintain priests and clerks.
Each human virtue, consider who can
Is pleasant to God and thankful to man,
And he that by grace of the Holy Ghost
To any one virtue is moved most.
Yet your virtue is seen in such guise
That each other's virtue you plainly despise.
Who would walk your way for God would find Him
The further they seek Him ever further behind him.
One kind of virtue to despise another
Is just as a sister should hang a brother.

POTH (*not flattered by the short sermon*): For fear such words on
    me should fall,
    I thank God I use no virtue at all!

PED (*turning on him*): That is of all the very worst way!
    For the harder it is, as I have heard say,
    To begin virtue where none is pretended
    Than where it begins with an abuse to be mended.
    Here, I suppose, you did say true
    When you said you use no virtue.
    In those very words, I dare well report,
    You are well beloved of all this sort
    By your railing here openly
    At pardons and relics so loudly.

POTH: In that I think my fault not too great
    For all his relics are but counterfeit.

PED: For his and all other you know to be feigned,
    You are neither told nor constrained
    To any such thing in any such case
    To give any reverence in any such place,
    But where you doubt the truth, not knowing,
    But believe ever the best, for good may be growing.

POTH: Go you before, and, as I am true man,
    I will follow as fast as I can.

PEDLAR *and* POTHECARY *slowly leave the stage.*
PARD: And so will I; he has said so well
Reason wishes we should follow counsel.
PARDONER *follows the others and leaves.* PALMER *closes the play.*
PALM: Then to our reason may God give us grace,
That we may follow with faith so firmly
His commandments that we may purchase
His love, and so consequently
To believe his Church fast and faithfully.
This was the reason the poet did make it,
And so we humbly beseech you to take it.
Beseeching Our Lord to prosper you all
In the faith of His Church Universal.
He bows and leaves the stage.

JACK JUGGLER

AN ANONYMOUS COMEDY

CHARACTERS

MASTER BONGRACE, *a gentleman*
DAME COY, *his wife*
JACK JUGGLER, *a knave*
JENKIN CAREAWAY, *a pageboy*
ALISON TRIP-AND-GO, *a maid*

SCENE: an open street with a single house. Entrances left and right.

JACK JUGGLER

This comedy was written about 1553 and has been attributed to
Nicholas Udall, Headmaster of Eton College. The central idea
is an amusing one. Jenkin Careaway is deluded by Jack Juggler,
a perfect twin for himself, who comes out of the same house that
Jenkin works in. Jenkin's part can be made a most rewarding
one. He is, of course, the Fool. He can offer small snatches of
female impersonation and can sustain his part in the brawl with
skill. But at the same time he is pleased to be what he is: a page
in the household of Master Bongrace. Although he exaggerates
the things that go wrong like the small boy that he is, it is quite
clear that many things go right; before we ever see him we know
him for an agile little fellow. In his last few lines we hear of the
carefree open-air life he enjoys. If he loses money he will get
more, and if he takes over an hour on an errand he is not afraid
to be criticized.

Jenkin is glad he is Jenkin, and why not? We are usually
proud of being who we are: our identity is important to us. Then,
suddenly and without due reason, somebody spies upon him,
dresses exactly like him and pretends to be him. How on earth
could we really prove our identity if somebody else arrived and
managed to support his claims with a good deal of evidence?
If this is what you find to be the play's meaning then it is not
entirely carefree: it is comic only up to a point.

Jack Juggler is a person we know nothing about. He comes out
of nowhere dressed like somebody else. We are amused by all
the word tangles that he causes over 'I-he' and 'him-me' but he
is a knave who has sport with an attractive innocent – as the
Epilogue points out. The answer to the question of his identity
is unexpected: he may be the god Mercury. This comes from a
Latin play on the same subject, *Amphitryon* by Plautus, in which

Mercury taunts a man named Sosia. Mercury is the god of thieves, amongst other things, the god of elusive people like Jack Juggler. The trick that Jack plays is taken from the Latin work, which Udall would have known.

The acting of this Interlude should be as dexterous as possible. The stage may be totally empty, though a doorway might be usefully designed on one side. All the centre of the stage is the street, and because the audience is drawn most uncomplimentarily into the text, the principals can come as near the spectators as the stage allows. *Jack Juggler* is particularly suitable for acting by children, and even though the main parts are those of Jack and Jenkin, the others are not without attraction and subtlety.

In the closing line of the sixteenth-century text there is an indication that the play was originally given as part of an indoor Christmas entertainment. The author wrote:

> I pray God grant and send many a good new year.

This we have slightly altered to be appropriate for acting at other times.

The Epilogue may be spoken by a new member of the cast or, as indicated, doubled by Bongrace. It may, if wished, be omitted altogether as it is not essential. There is, in the original text, a learned Prologue with a number of Latin quotations, which has also been omitted. However, five lines of it may be restored here as a prologue for this or any of the comedies in the book:

> Wherefore this writer delights passing well
> To follow his arguments and draw out the same,
> For to make at seasons convenient pastimes, mirth and game
> So now he has done this matter, not worth an oyster shell,
> Except perchance it shall fortune to make you laugh well.

JACK JUGGLER *saunters on to the stage from the street (stage left) and ambles towards the audience, if possible, performing a few juggling tricks.*

I am called Jack Juggler by many a one:
Indeed, I will play a juggling part anon.
I hope you may know good Master Bongrace,
The gentleman that lives here in this place.
And Jenkin Careaway his page, as cursed a lad
And right ungracious as ever good man had.
This Jenkin and I have fallen out of late
From an old cause that times does not abate.
Oh, I shall set but little on my wit
If I cannot with Jenkin this night be quit.
It chanced today at the end of the street
That with Jenkin and Bongrace I was forced to meet;
He imitates actions as he speaks.
Jenkin was prancing and springing in his short coat,
And pleasantly singing with a merry note.
'Hey, whither so fast? wait a little,' said one.
'I cannot now,' said Jenkin, 'I must now be gone.'
'My master sups near by at a gentleman's place;
I must take along there my dame, Mistress Bongrace.'
Yet he stopped half an hour or a little less
And then he was off to fetch his mistress.
But on the way he met with a fruiterer's wife,
And Jenkin and she fell into such strife
From snatching at apples, that down he cast
Her basket and gathered the fruit fast,
Filled up his sleeve and went on his way
By another lane as fast as he may.

Reveals apples in his own sleeve, takes them out and juggles with them.

> Then I passed by and it called into my mind
> Certain old reckonings, not far behind,
> Between Jenkin and me. These I would recompense
> By the good God's grace before I go hence.
> These garments, cape and other gear
> That now you see upon me here
> I have put on all like to his
> Today, and if you ask what my purpose is:
> I would make him believe, if only I can,
> That he is not himself, but another man.
> His mistress, I know, she will give him much blame;
> His master, also, will do much the same.
> So, as I have spoken he soon will be here;

He begins looking for his quarry.

> But now, I believe, I do his voice hear.

JACK *goes inside the house (stage right) just as* JENKIN CAREAWAY *comes to the centre of the stage from the left.*

JENKIN: My name is Jenkin Careaway, let all sorrow pass.
> I will tomorrow be as rich as I was,
> Though I have been away at a feast
> And lost two shillings and sixpence at the least.
> My mistress is, like all others, you see,
> A cursed shrew, by the blessed Trinity.
> A real devil, too, for if she once do begin
> To fight and chide, she will not cease her din.
> We always call her at home Dame Coy,
> A pretty but prickly one, God save her and St Loy.[1]
> As dainty-precise as a ha'pennyworth of silver spoons,
> But vengeful when melancholy most afternoons.
> A very great pleasure she takes of late
> To catch poor me now and then by the pate.

[1] St Loy was so mild that to swear by him was negligble. The Prioress in Chaucer's *Canterbury Tales* also swore by him.

My master himself is worse than she
When he once gets cross and heated at me.
He now imitates female movements.
    A maid too we have at home, Alison Trip-and-Go;
Not all London can show such a so-and-so.
She simpers, she pranks and struts without fail
Like a peacock that spreads out its gay tail.
She minces, she bridles, she swims to and fro,
She treads, no hair out of place, and trips like a doe.
A spiteful lying girl, and never well,
Except she some ill tale on me can tell.
I must call, for my master sent me for my lady,
And on my way here I have not been too hasty.
He knocks the door.
    Nobody comes out; can nobody hear?
He knocks again; JACK JUGGLER *answers.*
JACK: Soft your knocking, saucy knave, what make you here?
JENKIN (*aside*): What villain is that? Who speaks to me rough
      words so?
When we two meet one is like to feel a sharp blow.
And truly if I had a knife,
This rogue should hardly escape with his life.
I will teach him to ask any more
What I do at my own master's door.
JACK: If you but come from that gate, fool, knave,
I will lug you by the ears, as God me save!
JENKIN (*puzzled*): Will the monster show fight, by my honesty?
I know of no quarrel he has to me.
JACK: His back trembles now, and who chances to feel,
Shall find his heart creeping out at his heel;
Or else hidden in some part of his hose,
If it has not already dropped out of his nose.
Knock at the gate smartly again, if you dare,
And seeing that you will not of my words take care,
Now, I recall that just one week past

Four men asleep at my feet did you cast.
So, hands, belabour him about lips and face,
And strike out his teeth without any grace.
He spits on his palms and clenches his fists.
　Young sir, are you disposed towards some fist-meat?
JENKIN (*uneasily*): I have supped, I thank you, and seek not to
　　eat.
　Give it to them that are hungry, if you are wise.
JACK: It shall do a man of your size no harm to sup twice;
　It shall be like cheese to make meat digest,
　For, I tell you, these hands weigh of the best.
He now paces towards Jenkin and threatens him.
JENKIN (*terrified*): I shall never escape; how he trembles his hands
　He will use them upon me; I see how he stands.
Plucking up courage to address his opponent.
　Now, have you any just quarrel with me?
JACK: Before we two part, that will I show thee.
JENKIN: By my faith, if you are angry without a cause,
　You shall have amends made with a couple of straws.
　May a man demand whose servant you can be?
JACK: My master's servant I am, indeed, verily.
　I am commanded for to watch with diligence
　That in my good Master Bongrace's absence,
　No misfortune may befall his house, certain.
JENKIN: Good, now I am come, you may go off again,
　And thank them that so much for my master have done;
　Showing that the servants of the house have come home,
　For I am of this house and now in will I go.
JACK: I cannot tell whether you are of the house or no.
　Now, so God me snatch, if you go not away
　While you may, for a good forty day
　I shall make you unable to go or to ride
　But in a dung-cart or wheelbarrow on your side.
JENKIN: But my master has sent me home with a message—
JACK: Get off and walk; here is no passage.

Here my master and I have our habitation
And have always lived, each in his station,
At least a dozen years and odd
And here shall end our lives, by the grace of God.
He stands firm and blocks the way.

JENKIN: In the Father's name, what has come to pass?
For a while before supper here *our* house was,
And this day in the morning I will readily swear
That *my* master and I both dwelled here.

JACK: Who is your master? Tell me without lie,
And your own name add to it, and that shortly.

JENKIN: My master's name is Master Bongrace:
I have dwelled with him a long space,
And I am Jenkin Careaway his page.

JACK: What, you drunken fool, in your madness you rage.
Take that! (*Strikes Jenkin*) Are you Master Bongrace's page
And is Master Bongrace your master, do you still say?

JENKIN: I will swear on the book, he *was* early to-day.

JACK: You should somewhat more punishment have
Because you presumed like a lying knave
To say my master is yours. Who is your master now?
He strikes Jenkin still more fiercely.

JENKIN: Indeed, good sir, whosoever please you;
I am your own for you do beat so
As no man but a master should do.
(*Tearfully*) But save my life, help, or I am slain.

JACK: What, are you at your loud hollering again?

JENKIN: In faith, I have ceased crying: I will cry no more; *help,
help*!

JACK: Who is your master?

JENKIN: Master Bongrace.

JACK: I will make you change your song in this place,
For he is my master, and again I do say,
It is *I* who am his page Careaway.
Who are you then? (*He threatens him again*)

Now tell me quite plain.

JENKIN: Whoever you please, yes, certain—

JACK: You said even now your name was Careaway.

JENKIN: I cry you mercy, sir, and for pity I pray:
  I said it wrong because it *was* so early to-day,
  I hoped it should have continued alway.
  Like a fool as I am, and a drunken knave,
  You can see quite plain all the wit I have.
  Now I beseech you hold me no more to blame
  But find me a new master and another name.
  It would grieve the heart in this my poor body
  To run round the streets a masterless noddy.

JACK: I am he you said you were,
  And Master Bongrace is my master that dwells in here.

JENKIN: Oh, sir, might I be bold to say but one thing,
  Without any blows and without your beating?

JACK (*holding one hand up*): Truce for a while;
  Speak again if you must.

JENKIN: May a man in honesty by your word trust?
  I pray you swear by the mass you will do me no ill.

JACK: By my faith, I promise and pardon I will.

JENKIN *muses to himself and the audience*:
  Went not I with my master to-day
  In the early morning to the tennis play?
  At noon while my master at his dinner sat
  Played I not dice at a gentleman's gate?
  Did not I wait on my master to supper-ward?
  Sure I think I was not changed on my way homeward,
  Or else, if you think that I lie,
  Ask in the street among the passers-by.
  I remember I was sent to fetch my mistress,
  And what I devised to do, all harmless.
  Do I not speak now? is not this *my* hand?
  Did not this other knave knock hard on my head
  And beat me, I know, till I feel quite dead?

How can it be then that he should be I
And not I myself? It is a shameful lie.
I will home to our house, let no-one say nay,
As sure as my name is Jenkin Careaway.
(*To Jack*) Except that you tell me what you have done
Ever since five o'clock of this afternoon
Repeat it to me without a word of a lie,
Only then will I confess that you must be I.

JACK (*with a growing sense of superiority*): When my master came
    to the gentleman's place
He commanded me 'run home at a fast pace',
But I came by a wife that did apples there sell
And knocked down her basket, quick, smart and well,
I gathered as many as I could get
To stuff in my sleeve and here they are yet!

*He pulls them out of his sleeve once more and juggles with them to
Jenkin's mystification.*

JENKIN: How the devil did they come there
For I did them all in my own sleeves bear?
(*Aside*) He lies not a word in all this,
Nor does he in any single point miss. (*Scratches head*)
For all I can say in earnest or in game
I must go find me another name.
(*To Jack*) Yet you might have seen – say what followed behind.
Somehow I am sure I a liar can find.

JACK: I ran off homeward a different way,
But whether I stopped or not I will not say.

JENKIN (*comes closer to Jack*): Now, I do pray you, let no man
    hear,
But tell it all secretly in my own ear.

JACK (*whispers*): You lost all your money at dice and did curse,
Though you had picked it before from another man's purse.

JENKIN (*as if stung*): Oh, monstrous thief, who told you the same
A devil is speaking within you! How you defame!

JACK: Yes, see, I tell you Careaway is my name.

JENKIN (*raises hands*): And by these ten bones mine is the same,
    Or else pray tell me, if I am not he,
    What henceforth might my name now be?
    I see it is so without any doubt,
    But how the devil did this come about?
    Whoso in England looks on him and on me
    Shall perceive plainly Jenkin is he,
    He has in every point my clothing and gear,
    My head and my cap, my shirt and my hair;
    And of the same colour: my eyes, nose and lips,
    My cheeks, chin, neck, feet, legs and hips.
    Of the same stature and height and age
    And is in every point Master Bongrace's page.

He is now bewildered as he registers all these details and sits down disconsolate.

    Oh, when I remember I know not well how
    The same man I have ever been I think I am now;
    I know my master and his house; my wits still I have,
    So, why should I give belief to this knave?
JACK: Think you I have said all this in a game?
    Go, or I shall pack you off in the devil's name.
    Away, you hideous yob, you horrible slave,
    That your name does not know and no master can have.
JENKIN: Then, master, I do beg you, pray take the pain
    If I be found in any place, bring me to me back again.
Rises and addresses the audience.
    Have any of you heard of such a thing heretofore?
    No, nor ever shall, I daresay, from henceforth any more.
JENKIN *slowly leaves the stage and* JACK *watches him go.*
JACK: While he muses and judges and utters his moan
    I will steal away a while and leave you alone.
Exit JACK.

JENKIN *reappears cautiously.*

JENKIN: Good Lord of heaven, where did I myself leave,
　　Or who did me of my name on the way here bereave?
　　For I am sure of this in my own mind
　　That I did in no place leave myself all behind,
　　If I had played my name away with the dice
　　Or sold myself to any man at a price,
　　Or had made a brawl and lost it in fighting
　　Or had it stolen away while I was sleeping,
　　It would have been quite fair and I would have been patient
　　But here I am mad to have lost it in a mad moment.
　　Any man, sure, will see I am an idiot goose
　　Who would lose his ten toes if they hung loose.

Looks round the stage for Jack.

　　Where is that other I, oh, where is he gone?
　　To my master, by our Lord and St John,
　　Either to put me out of my place,
　　Or accuse me to my good master Bongrace.
　　But I will after, as fast as I can flee
　　And I trust to be there as soon as he.

A noise is heard as DAME COY *and* ALISON TRIP-AND-GO *enter
from the house.*

JENKIN (*shrinking into a corner*): I would go now, but I hear my
　　　mistress.
　　I shall never escape hanging. Here comes more distress.

COY (*in great fury*): I shall not sup this night, well I can see
　　For as yet there is nobody back to fetch me.
　　Of all unkind churlish husbands he is my last,
　　To let his wife sit here at home and still fast,
　　While he has gone out and stays to make cheer
　　With never a thought for his wife who stays here.

I shall shake him and berate in such a sort
He will fine me a medicine naught to his comfort.

ALISON: If I may be so bold, you may Page Jenkin thank
For I know he plays many a like prank.
For if you command him to go speak with some one
It is a full hour that he will be gone.
He will run forth and play in the street
Then he will say that no man can he meet.

COY: Nay, nay, that he has learned from his master's way,
He serves me so almost every third day.
But I will be even with him, as I hope to have joy –
Though the fault may indeed be all in the boy.

JENKIN *hearing this, tries to worm out of sight.*

JENKIN: Would to the Lord I could get out of her sight,
For I know by her look she is ready to fight!
Indeed she has on her angriest look.

COY: So there he is, that hideous crook.

JENKIN: God save me, mistress, do you know me so well?

COY: Come nearer, you villain, and then I shall tell.
You villainous rascal, now, is this at all wise
To make fun of your mistress and take a rise?
(*Striking him*) Take that for a start, and here is one more,
When your master comes home you must indeed start to roar.

JENKIN *tries to ward off the blows.*

JENKIN: Oh, stop, mistress; if you knew as much as I
You would not be half so rough and angry.
The fault is neither in my master, me, nor you,
But in another knave that was here just now
And said his name was Jenkin Careaway.

COY: So that is the trick that you intend to play!
You are drunken or mad, I cannot but vow.
My supper is lost and it is you who know how.

JENKIN: Yes, but on the way I had a great fall,
And my name, body, shape, my legs, head and all
Were taken by one who from me did them steal,

And he and I did blows to each deal.
If he were back again before your gate
You should pummel *him* swiftly about the pate.
COY: Oh, you stupid boy, do you stand there and mock
   To try and make of me a pure laughing-stock?
   Before you go out of here you shall have something
   And I will repeat the course in the morning.
JENKIN: And if you beat me, on body, head and brow,
   I say I am none of your servants now.
   That other I is now your page,
   It is with him that you must go and rage.
COY: Walk off, you idiot boy, away from my sight!
   Come into my sight no more this night.
DAME COY *and* ALISON *sweep out in annoyance.*
JENKIN (*to audience*): I would I had been hanged, I feel so lost.
   I have never been so worried and tossed.
   And if my master, for his part also,
   Handle me as my mistress and the other I do,
   I shall surely be killed between them three
   And all the devils in hell will never save me.
Exit slowly away from the house. JACK JUGGLER *appears from within.*
JACK (*to audience*): Have I not handled him after a good sort?
   Had it not been a pity to have lost such sport?
   I would not for the whole of a wine tun
   That any part of this had been undone.
   But now I have revenged my old quarrel
   I will take off this borrowed apparel.
He takes off some of his top garments.
   Now let Jenkin be Jenkin again;
   I have done with his name, certain.
He follows Jenkin into the town capering and laughing as he goes.

BONGRACE *enters, dragging Jenkin along with him. They halt before*
the house.

BONGRACE: Oh, you wicked rogue, dare you affirm to me
Something never seen nor ever could be:
That one man at one time may be in two places,
And bear with him two bodies and two faces?
Tell me, what did you drink on the way?

JENKIN: Nothing at all: there is no more I can say.
But as for you, if you gave me drink and meat
As oftentimes as you do me beat,
I were the best-fed pageboy in all this city:
But on that score you show me no pity.

BONGRACE: Why, you rascal and wicked rogue and knave,
How dare you stand there and shout and rave!
Your tongue wags too free and is much to blame.
I shall need now to beat you to make it more tame.
Where is that Jenkin you said also was here?

JENKIN: Now, by my soul, sir, he is nowhere.

BONGRACE: You do not think it was your shadow?

JENKIN: How could a shadow have beaten me so?

BONGRACE: On this I would a good sum and wager lay
That you lay down and slept by the way
And dreamed all this nonsense that you have told.

JENKIN: Oh, master, it all happened as I did unfold.
I had no sooner stepped up to knock at this gate
When this other *I* hit me hard on the pate.
I would to you on the good book now swear
That he had been watching out for me there,
For hours hidden in some secret place
To leap out and strike when he saw my face.
But where he is now cannot be far from hence:

He looks round the stage and into the audience.
　　Among this company, I will lay forty pence.
BONGRACE: Look round and see, go and smell him out,
　　Or I shall rap you on your lying slave's snout.
　　I will not be deluded with such a great lie,
　　Now will I believe till I see with my own fair eye.
JENKIN: Truly, good, sir, by your mastership's favour,
　　I cannot find out a knave by his savour.
　　Many here smell strong, but none so rank as he:
　　A worse-stinking knave there cannot be.
　　But here he was in that place there just now
　　And vanished suddenly, I know not how.
BONGRACE: Plainly it was your shadow that you did see,
　　For no other thing was it possible, to be.
JENKIN: But, I pray you, sir, by your good leave,
　　I know it was I by the apples in my sleeve.
He draws out apples from his sleeve.
　　He had the hair, the cap, the hose and the coat,
　　And in everything else like as fourpence to a groat.
　　He called himself by my own name
　　In every way he was precisely the same.
　　He told me all that I have done
　　Since five o'clock this afternoon:
　　How I scattered a basket of apples from a stall
　　And gathered them into my sleeve, one and all.
BONGRACE: So that is the guise of a trusty boy page
　　To play when he is sent out on a message!
BONGRACE *begins to beat* JENKIN *who hollers.* DAME COY *returns
at this point with a long stick.*
COY: Bang his head on a post; hurt not your own hand,
　　But lay about his ribs with this wand!
JENKIN: Mercy, mercy, mercy, I pray of you twain!
　　Save my life or, sure, I soon shall be slain!
　　I have had one beating enough for one day.
　　Oh, a mischief take that other *me* Careaway.

Is not this *he-I* a miserable knave
That will no more pity on *me-him* have.

COY: I knew it was true and said so just now
That no fault in all this could lie, dear, with you.
Truly, I have in you a great treasure
And you do all you can to give me great pleasure.

BONGRACE: I am sorry indeed that your luck has been ill,
And I would be gladly unsupped, so you had your fill.
Now go we in, sweetheart, that you may sup,
But you have cause to thank this stupid young pup.
Had Jenkin not been here you had fared very well.

COY: I bequeathe him a hot vengeance from the devil in hell.

MASTER BONGRACE *and* DAME COY *go into the house.*

JENKIN (*To audience*): Sirs, she lives in most charitable fashion
And all the year long is in such a passion.
But, masters, if you happen to see that other *I*,
I fear that you will, it is highly unlikely.
It is not like myself to run out from here
And miss all the best in this time of the year,
When honey lies in the hives of the bees
And the fruit falls down out of the trees,
As apples, nuts, pears and plums too,
Whereon a boy may live a month or two.

He moves over towards the house.

But now I will shut the gate and get me to bed,
For I promise you I have a most giddy old head.
And for you also, masters, I think it best
You go to bed too and take your good rest.
For which of you had been handled as I have been
Would out of his bed so long be seen?
So then, no more, I will steal out of sight
And I pray God give you all a very good night.

Exit.

EPILOGUE

MASTER BONGRACE *returns to deliver the closing speech.*[1]

Such is the fashion of the world nowadays,
That the simple innocents are confused
And in a hundred thousand different ways
By subtle and crafty means shamefully abused.
By strength, force and violence oft times compelled
To believe and say the moon is made of green cheese,
Or come to great harm, lose life and ease.
He must say he did amiss, though he did never offend;
He must beg forgiveness, where he did no trespass,
Or else be in trouble, care and misery without end,
And be lost in misery without hope of grace.
He that is stronger, more of power and might,
If he be disposed to revenge his cause,
Will pick a quarrel, be it wrong or right,
With the inferior or weaker for a couple of straws
And will against him so extremely lay down the laws,
That he will bring him to the worst, either by false injury,
Or by some craft and subtlety or else by plain tyranny.

As you saw just now by example plain
Another fellow, being a pretended page,
Brought the silly young servant quite out of his brain
And made him grant that he was fallen into dotage,
Feeling that in madness he had fallen a stage.
Therefore happy are they, that can beware
Into whose hands they fall by any chance;
Or if they once learn to escape from all care,
Trouble, misery and woeful grievance.

[1] If it is desired, the Epilogue may be spoken by a different performer,
or it may be omitted entirely.

Thus make I an end, committing you to his guidance
That made and redeemed us all, and to you that be here
I pray God grant and send many happy long year.
He bows and goes indoors.

JOHN JOHN, TIB AND FATHER JOHN

CHARACTERS

JOHN JOHN, *the husband*
TIB, *his wife*
FATHER JOHN, *the curate*

SCENE: open stage; on one side John's house, on the other, the priest's house. Entrances right and left.

JOHN JOHN, TIB AND FATHER JOHN

The full title of this was originally *John John the husband, Tib his wife, and Sir John the Priest*. The source from which Heywood obtained a good deal of his material was a French farce called *Farce du Pasté* (The Play of the Pie).

Heywood's plot is extremely simple. A pie has been made as a token by a little circle of village women and the priest, and it is to be eaten by Tib and the priest alone. It is clearly not intended that John John shall have any part of it, but it is not possible to exclude him from the party altogether. The writer set himself the task of keeping John employed while allowing him to see his wife's unfaithful behaviour. There is no reason for him to sit by the fire all the time melting the wax he needs to mend the pail in which he is to fetch water. It must be shown that it is fear of his wife that keeps him from joining the meal at the table. It is the essence of good comedy, however, for him to have to call on his rival, the priest, with an invitation to the supper at which he is actually the uninvited host.

Each of the characters is now on the defensive, now on the offensive; now telling the truth, now telling lies. John John himself is a boaster at the start; then a coward; finally he takes the stage and shows his paces as a wife-beater and priest-beater into the bargain. Tib has great spirit and should be genuinely lively in her manner. She may actually feel sick for a moment, and she asks for sympathy from her husband. At the end of the play, she is simply the unfaithful wife. Father John is a figure of amusement because he is a clergyman. Had he been the village baker the humour would not have been the same, for there would then have been no ridicule of authority. In spite of his comic aspect, Father John's explanations (though lies) are perfectly convincing to his hearer.

In acting the Interlude, care should be taken not to rush the action. The dialogue should stop if necessary, to give time to acting and then should be resumed as naturally as possible. Generally speaking, each of the actors has a considerable task, to portray a number of shifts in character.

Tib and the clergyman share a wonderful opportunity for making much of their pie-eating. It can be shown as a little love-feast with the two diners glancing at each other, engrossed in each other's company, brushing aside John John when he joins in the grace and tries to approach the table.

The staging is not difficult to devise. There should be doors for two houses, and stretching across the back, the fireplace. A trestle-table needs to be put up during the course of the action and a few other domestic items should be brought on to establish the scene. The front of the stage is to be kept for solo speeches and there is no reason why John John and Father John should not circle the whole of the stage to represent the journey fron one house to the other.

Enter JOHN JOHN, *the husband, (stage left).*

JOHN JOHN (*to audience*): God speed you, masters, every one;
    Know you not whither my wife has gone?
    I pray God the devil take her!
    For all that I can do I cannot make her
    Do anything but go gadding far too much –
    Like an Anthony pig[1] with an old witch,
    That leads her about hither and thither.
    But, by Our Lady, I never know whither.
    I am even mad that I beat her not now;
    But I shall reward her, and that I do vow.
    There's never a wife between heaven and hell
    Who was ever beaten one half so well.
Picks up a stick and advances towards the audience.
    But, masters, for God's sake, do not entreat
    For her when she shall be beat;
    But, for God's passion, just let me alone
    And I shall thwack her hard till she shall groan:
    Head, shoulders, arms, legs and all,
    I shall beat her – I tell you I shall.
Searches in various directions and looks off-stage.
    But where the devil, now, can she be gone?
    I bet a noble she's with the priest, Father John.
    Sure, I think, wherever she does go,
    Many an honest wife goes thither also.
    If I forbid Tib to go there any more,
    Yet she will be off as she did before.
    Or else they will meet in some other place,
    And the matter would still be an awkward case.

[1] A pig thought to be a familiar spirit for a witch.

When she comes home she will begin to chide
And shall have payment upon the backside.

Enter TIB *carrying a basket, speaking menacingly, from the right.*

TIB: Why, whom will you beat, I say, you great knave?

JOHN: Who, I, Tib? No one, God me save.

TIB: But I heard you say you wanted to beat—

JOHN: Nay, wife, to eat dried fish from Thames Street,
Which will be good food during Lent.
Why, Tib, what did you think I meant?

Retreats to fireplace at back.

TIB: Indeed, I thought I did hear you bawling.
Will you never stop your hideous brawling?

JOHN: What, wife, what's this? Was it not clever of me
To know you would be home maybe
As soon as I had kindled a fire?
Come warm yourself, love, that I desire.

Sits down by fire.

TIB: Oh, John John, I am afraid, by this light,
That I shall be sore sick all this long night.

JOHN JOHN *paces angrily towards the audience.*

JOHN (*to audience*): By God's soul, now, I dare wager a swan
That she comes now straight from Father John,
For when she has been out, I see the trick,
She comes home and then says she feels sick.
If our parish priest, Father John,
Did not see her now and then
And give her absolution upon her bed,
For woe and pain she would soon be dead.

TIB: For God's sake, John John, I beg you, please,
Many a time I am ill at ease.
Am not I now truly somewhat sick?

JOHN (*aside, threateningly*): Now would to God I had my heaviest
stick,
Or you were in the water up to your throat,
Or in a burning oven all over red hot

To see if I would come pull you out.

Returns to the fire and sits.

TIB: Imagine where an hour ago I was –
      Before I came home?

JOHN: You were praying in the Church of St Paul's,
      Upon your knees, for all us Christian souls?

TIB: No – but truly John, we made a pie,
      I and my gossip Margery,
      And our gossip dear, Father John,
      And my neighbour's youngest daughter, Anne;
      The priest paid for the stuff, and the making,
      And Margery provided for all the baking.
      Now, by my soul, I never go to Father John
      But I find him a true holy person,
      For he is either saying his devotion
      Or else he is going in procession.
      But that pie that was made I now have here,

Produces pie from basket.

      And I trust we shall now be of good cheer.

JOHN: By God's body, that makes me happy.

TIB: You know who did give it?

JOHN: What the devil care I?

TIB: By my faith, I must tell you then –
      The devil take me – it was Father John.

JOHN: That pie will come to no harm;
      Let us set it down on the hearth to warm.

Places it before fire.

TIB: And let us eat it as soon as we can.
      But Father John is so honest a man
      That I wish that he could eat his part.

JOHN: There is good reason, I am sure.

TIB: Then since that is your pleasure,
      I pray you go to him straight
      And beg him come sup with us tonight.

JOHN (*aside*): Is he coming here? I was plainly accursed

When I gave in so quickly at first.
But since I've said it, I dare not say nay,
For then my wife and I would make an affray.
But when he is come, I swear by God's mother,
I will bid the devil take one or the other.

TIB: What do you say?

JOHN (*uneasily*): Marry, he is the priest, I say,
My confessor and my friend in every way.
But go you and ask him, bring him now, say I,
And till you come back, I will watch the pie.

TIB: No, you must go tell him – you do that.

JOHN: Then what do I tell him; tell me what?
That you want him along to make good cheer?

TIB: No, that *you* desire him to come and sup here.
(*Aside*) I see my husband will often prate
For this invitation to our gentle curate.

JOHN: What did you say? Let me hear it again.
(*Aside*) That monster, that haunter of vice,
Knave who seeks all women to entice;
Liar, wretch, and maker of strife,
Shall he lay his hands on my dear wife?

TIB: What was that, what have you said?

JOHN: That I would like our table set and laid,
On this side or the other. (*Pacing about stage*)

TIB: Then go on, bring the trestles hither.
Wait a while, let me take off my gown.

Goes to put it by the fire
Yet I am afraid to lay it down:
If I lay it on the hearth bare,
It might be chanced to be burned, and I unaware.
Therefore I beg you (*to a member of the audience*), will you take
  the pain
Of keeping the gown till I come back again.
But he is near the door, he might run away!

Turns to another member of the audience.

But because you look so trusty and sure,
You shall keep it, and if it give pleasure,
Because it is rather muddy at the skirt,
While you have nothing to do, scrape off the dirt.

JOHN (*having put up the table*): So, now I am ready to find Father
    John,
And bid him come here as fast as he can.
    (*Aside, going*) I pray to Christ, if my wish is no sin,
That the priest break his neck as soon as he comes in.
I go – and may a mischief alight on your face!

TIB: Go, and bid him hurry apace.
Meanwhile, I shall all things amend.

JOHN *crosses to the hearth.*

JOHN (*cynically*): The pie is burning here at this end.

TIB: On your way now, and tarry no more,
For I am hungered full sore.

Begins to push him out.

Are you still pottering about the place?
You could have gone and come back in all this space.

JOHN *crosses from his house to the priest's.*

JOHN: Now if my wife starts on her chiding,
It is time for me to go at her bidding.

TIB *prepares the table for dinner during John's absence, and when she
is finished, exit.*

SCENE II

JOHN *walks over to stage left and knocks on an imaginary door (the
sound of knocking coming from off stage).*

JOHN: How, master curate, may I come in?
FATHER J: Who is that now that would see me?
Makes to open door.
    Oh, John John! What news comes with thee?
JOHN: Marry, sir, to tell you shortly,

My wife and I pray you heartily,
And do desire you with all your might
To come over and sup with us tonight.

FATHER J: You must pardon me, I am not sure I can.

JOHN: Oh, I desire you to, truly, Father John,
Do this just once. And, to say the least,
If you will not do it at my own request,
Then do it, I beg, for the love of my wife.

FATHER J: I cannot go, it will only cause strife.
But I'll tell you what you can do;
You stay here and sup with me; do not go.

JOHN: You will not come then. I pray, why so?

FATHER J: To tell you the truth, between you and me,
Your wife's as wise a woman as can be.
I know it well, for I have had the charge
Of her soul, and searched her conscience at large.
I never knew her but honest and wise,
Without any malice or any vice.
But one fault I know in her, no more,
And because I rebuke her at times therefore,
She is angry with me and holds me in hate.
Yet what I do, I do for your wealth.

JOHN: Now the good God grant, master curate,
All you wish and may He send you health.

FATHER J: Now let me tell you; we sometimes go aloft,
And I have stayed with her many times and oft,
To test her, but I could never espy
That ever any did worse with her than did I.

JOHN: Sir, that is the least care I have out of nine.
Thanks be to God, and your good doctrine.
But, may it please you, tell me the matter
Which is at debate between you and her.

FATHER J: I shall tell you, but it must be secret.

JOHN: Tell it to me, Father, you shall not regret.

FATHER J: Then I shall tell you the matter plain;

She is angry with me and shows her disdain
Because I do her often entice
To do penance, and give her advice,
Because she will never stop her bawling.
With you she is always chiding and brawling.
I dare swear that she holds me in deep hate.

JOHN: No, I dare swear for her, master curate:
(*Aside*) But was I not a perfect knave?
I thought, surely, as God shall me save,
That he loved my wife, tried to deceive me;
But now he has explained, and here do I see,
He does as much as he may, in fear of his life,
To quell the debate between me and my wife.

FATHER J: If ever she did, or thought me any ill,
So now I forgive her of my own free will;
Therefore, John John, go get you back home
And thank your wife and say I cannot come.

JOHN: But let me know now, Father John,
Where you will go to supper anon?

FATHER J: Indeed I will – and this I can tell you:
On Saturday last, with friends one or two,
I made up a plan to keep an appointment.
So, for this night we all did assent
That in one place we would sup all together;
And one of them said that she would bring hither
Ale and bread; and for my part, I
Said that I would give them a pie.
And there I gave them money for the making –
Since another would provide for the baking.
And so we propose to make good cheer
And to drive away care and sad thought.

JOHN: But I pray you, sir, tell me here,
Whither should all this gear now be brought?

FATHER J: By my faith, indeed, I will not lie:
It was to go to your wife was that pie.

JOHN: By God, it is at my house in front of the fire.
FATHER J: Who ordered that pie? this I require.
JOHN: By my faith, and I shall not lie,
   It was my wife and her gossip called Margery,
   And your good worship, dear Father John,
   And my neighbour's youngest daughter, Anne;
   Your worship paid for the stuff and the making,
   And Margery, indeed, she paid for the baking.
FATHER J: If you will have me now, indeed I will go.
JOHN: Yes, marry, I beseech your worship, do so.
   My wife waits only now for us twain,
   And thinks I should long have been home again.
FATHER J: Well now, if she chides me in your presence,
   I will be content and bear it in patience.
JOHN: By the Lord's soul, if she once chides
   Or frowns, or lours, or looks aside,
   I shall bring you a staff as large as I can heave,
   Then beat her and spare not; I give you good leave.
They re-cross the stage to John's house.

SCENE III

Enter TIB.

TIB: There is not a spot of water, by my gown,
   To wash our hands with before we sit down.
   Go and speed you, as fast as a snail,
   And with clean water fill me this pail.
Gives her husband a pail and he begins to go.
FATHER J: Ah, good gossip, is that well said?
TIB: Welcome, my dearest sweetheart,
   We shall make cheer before you depart.
JOHN: God's soul, look how he approaches so near
   Unto my wife: this lessens my good cheer. (*Exit*)
TIB *and* FATHER JOHN *sit down.*

FATHER J: Dear God, I wish you had heard the trifles,
   The toys, mocks, fables – the pure piffles
   That I made your husband believe and think!
   You might almost into the hearth sink,
   You could not stop laughing for hours.
   But peace, the good man is back – how he lours!
Re-enter JOHN. *Pauses, seeing the two laughing together.*
JOHN: In God's name, what have we here?
   As far as I saw, he drew so near
   Unto my wife. . . .
TIB: What, are you back so soon?
   Give us the water to wash now – have done.
JOHN *reveals an empty pail to the audience and gazes into it forlornly.*
JOHN: In the Lord's name, it was full to the brink,
   And now it has gone before I could think.
   Oh, I see there is a hole, both large and wide.
   Look, wife, here it is on this side.
TIB: Why don't you stop it?
JOHN: Why, how shall I do it?
TIB: With a little wax.
JOHN: Where shall I get that?
FATHER J: Marry, here are two wax candles, I say,
   Which my friend Margery gave me but yesterday.
TIB: Oh, let him alone, for, by the rood,
   It is a pity to help him, or do him good.
FATHER J: Ho! John John, can you make no shift?
   Take this wax and stop the great cleft.
JOHN: The wax is as hard as any wire.
TIB: Then soften it a little there by the fire.
JOHN *is driven over to the fire.*
JOHN (*aside*): Oh, now God help me: here in my home!
   She is the wickedest bawd between here and Rome.
TIB: What did you say?
JOHN: Do take the pie, or I must turn,
   It a moment longer – else it will burn.

TIB: We shall start to sup, Father John and I.

JOHN: How now, what shall I do with the pie?
  Shall I not eat a single morsel?

FATHER J (*saying grace*): Benedicite . . .

JOHN (*joining in*): . . . Dominus.

He begins to approach the table but is turned back by TIB.
  Is this not a very purgatory?
  To see folk eat, but not myself to have any.
  What a vengeance on you both as you sit,
  For I know well I shall not eat a bit.

FATHER J (*eating*): Good John John, now I drink health to you.
  What cheer make you, from the fire as you view?

TIB: Here is good drink, and here our good pie.

FATHER J: We fare well. Blessed be Our Lady.

JOHN: Oh, now the smoke puts out my eyes too;
  My face burns and my clothes singe also.
  And yet I dare not say an angry word.
  While they sit laughing, the two at my board.

TIB: What is it now that makes you patter
  John John? What is it now that makes you chatter?

JOHN: I melt the wax, and make hard shift
  To stop herewith the pail's deep rift.
  (*Aside*) Look how that paltry priest crams it in;
  I wish to God that therewith he might choke.

FATHER J: That is the bond of wedlock and the yoke.
  You must do something at your wife's desire.
  You must stay there roasting by the hot fire.
  I know a man who had wedded a wife –
  As fair a woman as was ever alive –
  And within one week after, indeed very soon,
  He went overseas and left her alone.
  He tarried away for about seven year,
  And when he came homeward he had heavy cheer,
  For it was told him that he was in heaven.
  But when at the end to his home he did pace,

He found his wife and her children seven
Which she had had during that space;
Yet she would not have had so many as three
If she had come for some help to me.
Is this not a miracle, if ever there were any,
That this good wife should have children so many
Here in this town, while her husband should be
Beyond the sea, in a distant country?

JOHN: A miracle, yes; it is indeed quite wondrous.
  If I could steep your head – I feel so thundrous –
  Deep in scalding water! I would give you the rod!

TIB: Peace, I say; you do slander a minister of God.

FATHER J: Another miracle also is this:
  I knew another woman too, certain it is,
  Who was wedded and within five months after
  Was delivered of a perfect fair daughter,
  As well formed in every limb and joint,
  And as complete in every point.

TIB: Indeed, Father John, but yet for all that,
  I have seen the day that puss, my cat,
  Has had in a year kittens eighteen.

JOHN: Yes, Tib, dear wife; that have I seen.
  But say, Father John, was it good now, your pie?
  Not one morsel of it tasted I.
  It is eaten up, not left one bit,
  And you two together there do sit
  Eating and drinking at your own desire
  And I am John John who must stand by the fire.

TIB: Then we now rise up out of this place.

FATHER J: And kiss me then, instead of the grace;
  So farewell sweetheart and love so dear.

JOHN: But, dear wife, no food has come my way here.

TIB: What, not a morsel?

JOHN: No, not one bit.
  For hunger, I fear I shall fall in a swoon.

FATHER J: Have you not drunk?

JOHN: No, not a bit.

I warmed this wax in my hand,
As here by the fire I was forced to stand.
The smoke has put out my eyes too;
I have burned my face, and singed my clothes also,
Mending the pail which is rotten and old;
It can hardly stay together now and stand.
And since this is so, and since you twain
Would not give me meat, take the pail again,

Throws the pail at them.

And if you can mend it, then show me just how.

TIB: Oh, reach me my distaff, or by my clipping shears,
I shall make the blood trickle down from his ears.

JOHN: No, if you once stir toward this place

Picks up shovel.

I shall throw a shovel of coals in your face.

TIB: Oh, so? Your ears I will grab.

JOHN: No, then – get out of my house, you wretched priest's
drab.

FATHER J: You lie, you lie, cuckold, I spit in your face.

JOHN: And *you* lie, false priest, with your stories so base.

TIB: And *you* lie.

JOHN: And you lie, sir.

FATHER J: And you lie again.

TIB: At him, Father John, or God give you sorrow.

JOHN: And have at you two, St George to borrow!

They fight each other by the ears till the wife and priest rush out.
JOHN *takes the centre of the stage.*

JOHN: Ah, sirs, that was a scene I would never have missed!
I have paid them both with good blows from my fist.
I thank God I have walked them well
And driven them hence. But yet, can you tell
Where they have gone? For now, by God, I fear me
That they have gone together, he and she,

Back to his chamber; and perhaps she will,
In spite of her vows, tarry there still.
Then had I a pig in the wrong pannier.
So now, by God, I must follow thither
To see if they are now at such base villainy.
And so, fare well I say to this noble company.
Crosses to the priest's house in a hurry and exit.

APPENDIX

SOME NOTES UPON PRODUCTION

The scripts of these plays as they appear on the page are little more than their barest bones. Very few of us can visualize a play as we read it and not every production does more than scratch the surface. There is at once the danger, when dealing with period plays, that stage properties and costumes are allowed to take the place of imaginative production and intelligent pointing of the salient words in the dialogue. Though all too little is known about the actual presentation of such short plays in Tudor times, it is self-evident that with only a hall or the end of a great chamber to play in, the actors had to be content with simplicity. Interludes thrive, therefore, on a physical minimum combined with an artistic maximum: the best production will simply be that which helps the audience to get the dramatist's point. Children invariably help in this respect by bringing a spontaneous and at times a sobering atmosphere with them which animates or intensifies a production to the correct degree.

With *The Play of the Weather*, a suitable set need not be more than a raised platform with varying heights laid out as acting areas. Jupiter's throne should be set apart in some way. In *John John*, since most of the action takes place in one house, it can occupy three-quarters of the stage and the other houses can be compressed to a minimum. In early presentations we believe that a house may not have been more than a painted door. A small rostrum placed at an angle to the audience, approached if possible by a series of steps, would be of great value. Almost the same set, reduced to a single house, will be entirely adequate for *Jack Juggler*.

Properties required for these plays are symbolic rather than realistic. Thus, in order to suggest the church for *The Pardoner and the Friar* a lectern might be sufficient: the main actors then would be fighting over the right to use it. Personal properties have been suggested elsewhere for the actors in the *Four P's:* any step taken to differentiate this quartet will be of advantage to the audience.

Costumes are often a major difficulty. Modern dress may be defended on the score that such old plays are still alive and able to communicate. This, however, will not do for *Jack Juggler* where a harlequin element ought not to be missed and the items which are employed in dressing both actors are explained in the text. Elizabethan costumes, though a little late for chronological accuracy, will do well enough since in England we have come to take this period as the standard for historical dress.

In *The Play of the Weather* the element of social class appears and the brightest colours should be reserved for the gentry. It might not be impossible for the costume of Jupiter to suggest the famous portrait of Henry VIII as long as the audience is told the reason for the identification. Jupiter should not, on this occasion, look like a Greek god. Merry-Report needs the jester's dress with a motley colouring. Bright colours can be allowed, and there is nothing that a thoughtful producer will do that is likely to be completely out of key.

The standard work on the costume of the period is: C. W. and P. Cunnington, *Handbook of English Costume in the Sixteenth Century* (Faber). For theatrical costuming we might make mention of: L. Barton, *Historic Costume for the Stage* (A. & C. Black); Fernald and Shenton, *Costume Design & Making* (A. & C. Black). The original editions of old plays sometimes had pictures from which the costumes can be copied and the celebrated Ellesmere portrait miniatures of Chaucer's characters will give an idea of pardoners and friars that may be considered. The complete set of these appears in: Maurice Hussey, *Chaucer's World: A Pictorial Companion* (C.U.P.). While finally, for whatever is known about the performance of Interludes, the producer and student should turn to: T. W. Craik, *The Tudor Interlude* (Leicester University Press).

Lighting is a valuable aid to the producer and even the most meagre of lighting resources may be used to advantage. As an element of production lighting should not draw attention to itself, whereas it is expected that the audience should notice costumes and scenery. Spot-lights are therefore preferable to powerful floodlights or battens. The interaction of light on costumes must also be taken into account. It is a well-known function of colour that certain hues may suggest emotional or psychological states. *The Pardoner and the Friar* might be dimly lit as befits its setting in a medieval English church (whilst the Pardoner may be dressed in a grey robe and the Friar in brown). In contrast the more light-hearted *Jack Juggler* might be sunlit as should

The Four P's where the characters might be presented as in a market square. Two useful books on lighting are: G. Ost, *Stage Lighting* (Herbert Jenkins) and A. Wilson, *Stage Lighting for Amateur Production* (Pitman).

Since the original music is inaccessible we have been obliged to remove from our adaptations one or two songs and dances that appear in the texts. A drum-roll to introduce Jupiter, a jig to bring on Jack Juggler, are obvious enough, but if a producer has a musician to hand and a singer in the company there is no harm at all in introducing a song here and there, or for the quartet of P's to break into both song and dance.

All the Tudor Interludes involved the audience in some way or other: the actors looking out into their midst, coming up on to the stage and chatting to them on the way, or even being planted among them. If an open-air production is contemplated it would be quite permissible for the actors to be seated in the front row of the audience: they would rise and mount the stage at their cue, play, and having made their exit they would return to their place. An audience will not find such procedure distracting for dramatic illusion always wins through. On many occasions audiences were insulted, as they are here for being thieves and for their smell. Traditional circuses and pantomimes still do much the same, and with open stages and projecting platforms it was natural for an actor to talk familiarly to those nearest him. These plays always encourage such *rapport* between actor and audience. In this way a young actor will learn considerable confidence and these one-act comedies will be a useful stepping-stone to the acting of Shakespearean plays to which in the first instance they so happily led.